Throughout my career I have worked for a variety of small, medium, and large companies. I truly believe the skills taught in this book can be applied to any size sales team or sales industry. Take a step back, gain fresh insights—and immense success will follow.

> —Chad Heath
> Sales Manager, Stone Brewing Company

Just when I thought I had heard it all and seen it all, a new perspective on what it takes to be effective in the game of sales. This is a must-read for anyone who wants to excel in the sales profession. I highly recommend this book to any successful salesperson who wants to go to the next level.

> —Raoul Quintero
> President and CEO
> Maquet Cardiovascular

At the end of the day this book provides key insights into human fundamentals. It also provides a great platform for how to embrace change and win with your team—and your customers.

> —Tony Puckett
> President, Valvoline Instant
> Oil Change

This is now at the top of the list for my senior sales and management teams. It is sharp, witty, and relevant. The action plan is impressive in its scope and understanding of human nature at its best and worst.

> —Stu Gomm
> Vice President and
> General Manager, Arthrocare

We are in an economy that most of us have never experienced before. Only the best of the best will experience sustained success. This book should be a prerequisite for all 'top gun' sales reps and sales managers.

> —Gail Turner
> Division Manager, St. Jude Medical

What Got You Here Won't Get You There

in *Sales!*

How Successful Salespeople Take It to the Next Level

MARSHALL GOLDSMITH
DON BROWN · BILL HAWKINS

New York   Chicago   San Francisco   Lisbon   London   Madrid   Mexico City
Milan   New Delhi   San Juan   Seoul   Singapore   Sydney   Toronto

1 2 3 4 5 6 7 8 9 0   DOC/DOC   1 6 5 4 3 2 1

ISBN: 978-0-07-177394-2
MHID: 0-07-177394-0

e-ISBN: 978-0-07-177446-8
e-MHID: 0-07-177446-7

This publication is designed to provide accurate and authoritative information in regard to the subject matter covered. It is sold with the understanding that neither the author nor the publisher is engaged in rendering legal, accounting, securities trading, or other professional service. If legal advice or other expert assistance is required, the services of a competent professional person should be sought.
> —*From a Declaration of Principles Jointly Adopted by a Committee of the American Bar Association and a Committee of Publishers and Associations*

Library of Congress Cataloging-in-Publication Data
Goldsmith, Marshall.
    What got you here won't get you there in sales : how successful salespeople take it to the next level / by Marshall Goldsmith, Don Brown, Bill Hawkins.
    p. cm.
    Includes index.
    ISBN-13: 978-0-07-177394-2 (alk. paper)
    ISBN-10: 0-07-177394-0 (alk. paper)
    1. Selling. 2. Sales management. I. Brown, Don II. Hawkins, Bill III. Title.
    HF5438.25.G6425 2012
    658.85—dc23

                                                        2011018028

To those closest to us:

Marshall Goldsmith: Special accomplishments require the patience of spouses, family, and friends. Mine were no exception. A special thank-you to my wife, Lyda, daughter Kelly, and son Bryan. You help me keep perspective and make things fun! Thank you!

Don Brown: To Colleen, Natalie, Kelly, and Katie—you make me the richest man on earth. Thank you for being there, being patient, and being you. *Amor y besos.*

Bill Hawkins: Special thanks to my wife, Linda—the glue who holds the family together while I'm 30,000 feet in the air in another time zone. Your support, encouragement, and help on this book are appreciated. To my daughters, Sarah and Sandy, and son, Dave, I'm so proud of each of you. I love you very much.

Contents

Acknowledgments

A labor of love such as this book is always a team sport. We'd like to acknowledge the people who helped us find out what differentiates average sales interactions from the very best and helped us define and refine the 16 habits by providing examples, feedback, and support to keep us on track:

David Abeles, John Akers, Arbie Allen, Jeff Asmus, Paige Billings, Sam Brown, Steve Brown, Dean Bruce, Chris Coffey, Bob Colloton, Chris Cordero, Ron Curtis, Rich Daly, Mike Davison, Dave Furstoss, Alberto Galue, Jim Goodrich, John Halquist, Chad Heath, Tom Heinselman, Jamie Hinely, Jim Hobby, Maya Hu-Chan, John Kennedy, John Kilcoyne, Mark Koenig, Jack Lewis, Carlos Marin, Sarah McArthur, John McLean, Charlie Merchant, Jim Moore, Howard Morgan, Nancy Palmerin, Tony Puckett, Raoul Quintero, Chris Richardson, Linda Sharkey, Wendy Stapleford, Jim Vaughan, Frank Wagner, and Tony Welsh.

To you our readers, we wish many happy sales.

A Letter from Marshall Goldsmith

Don, Bill, and I share over 100 years of experience in the applied behavioral sciences, from earning advanced degrees to working in some of the most highly successful organizations on the planet (and some not-so-successful ones). The common thread that runs throughout our collective past is belief in the power and resilience of the human spirit. Whether coaching top executives or working with sales or service reps, we have come to the following seemingly irrefutable conclusions about the human condition:

1. **People quite naturally try to connect to other human beings** and under the right conditions do connect.
2. **People quite naturally exercise free will** and, given the proper methodology, can and do consciously change their predominant behavioral patterns.

A few years ago I published my bestseller *What Got You Here Won't Get You There*, which was written as a guide for today's managers to stopping the interpersonal habits that keep them from leading their organizations more effectively. At the same time, I was part of a review board for Don's research on the impact of coupling coaching follow-up with training in Situational Selling® (both Don and I had the blessing of a relationship with Paul Hersey as boss, mentor, friend, and significant life event). After reviewing some pretty phenomenal results in the research, I called Don and Bill Hawkins, who had spent decades managing sales organizations, and asked, "Do you guys want to do a book together?"

Couple a runaway bestseller approach with solid research at the line level of customer influence and a literature search of sales development over the last 50 years—and for balance add 100 years of hands-on experience—and you have *What Got You Here Won't Get You There in Sales!*

Life is good!

—MARSHALL

Introduction

What Got Us Here:
How We Know What to Stop

First of all, thank you for buying this book. If someone bought it for you, thank that person—you'll be glad he or she did, and your customers will be too. Our mantra "what got you here won't get you there" is all about accepting the fact that some of what worked in the past is going to fail in the future. Take a look on the cover—"The 16 Habits Your Customers Want You to Give Up." This is our approach—not what to do but what to *stop* doing to be more effective in sales and our methodology, as you'll see, is powerful.

But why should you listen? Why should you read on?

You should read on because there are two questions that are foundational to human skills development, and we can answer them in the affirmative:

1. Can people really change? Can we ever really achieve a lasting positive shift in our behavior?
2. Through changes in *individual* behavior, can we have an impact on the existing *organizational* metrics of sales and gross profit?

The answer to both questions is yes. We have clients who have documented positive lasting behavioral change across thousands of employees, and one of our clients reaped a return of $4,120 per sales professional from using our methods in training and follow-up. Our clients have harvested sales increases anywhere from 5 to 30 percent, along with gross profit increases of up to 50 percent on that revenue growth. What would that be worth to you? Here is what our research has taught us:

- There is a demonstrable connection between human skills development and bottom-line business results: Sales training can increase revenue.
- It is possible to measure the impact of the sales training dollars being spent, usually through existing organizational metrics.
- We can maximize the impact of sales training dollars by employing simple follow-up methods. Follow-up is not training. It is, however, the missing link that makes training worthwhile.
- Substantial gains can be realized through human skills development, yet many organizations lack the courage to measure and quantify that return.
- Peter Drucker is a hero of ours. We invoke his decree: "It is not whether an answer is right but whether it works."

What you will read in this book isn't right or wrong . . . but it works.

Happy sales!

What Got
You Here
Won't Get
You There
in
Sales!

The Millennial Challenge

Rules to play by . . . roles to clarify . . . what connects us . . . and a new *approach to change.*

- Discover the new work rules in our business environment and economic realities that won't go away.
- Accept the importance of empathy as the organic connection between all of us.
- Consider a new paradigm of personal change and growth: stopping ineffective habits and the damage they inflict.

Hi-Tech/No-Touch— The Game Changes Again

In 1987 Larry Wilson wrote his bestseller *Changing the Game* to let us know how the economy and our customers were experiencing unprecedented change—and how the game of selling needed to change to accommodate major shifts in decision making, sales cycles, a proliferation of events out of our control, and the pervasive demand for more and better solutions and relationships. Sound familiar? Here we are over 20 years later, and the world is even more complicated, competitive, and complex.

Well into the information age, we're again experiencing an accelerated pace of economic upheaval, with periods of calm few and far between. The selling context *has* changed, customers *are* different, and buying *is* different. Selling will continue to be more difficult. With much broader product lines, more complex product and service offerings, and companies jumping into new markets to survive, it is no wonder that it can take two years for a salesperson to ramp up to being productive. To learn what you need to know, meet who you need to meet, and close what you need to close, the average time it takes to get up to speed in sales is over seven months. Sales isn't just different, it's tougher than it has ever been.

Couple this with the fact that we have experienced what some would say is the most pervasive economic decline in living memory, and it is obvious that the game has changed again.

"IT'S THE ECONOMY, STUPID"

This is a phrase that was used heavily in American politics in 1992 as a way for the Clinton campaign to unseat George H. W. Bush (by the way, it was successful). In drawing attention away from Bush's strengths in foreign policy and instead focusing on the recession that had just ended and its lingering effects, the Democrats resonated with the electorate and were able to defeat a popular incumbent. The phrase resonates today as we enter the second decade of the twenty-first century; it is *still* the economy. The evolution of countries in the Middle East, natural disasters in Asia—everything has economic ramifications.

There are two key factors to consider in understanding the direction of our collective economy and therefore our challenges in the world of sales: employment and capacity. Let's take employment first. We recently lost some 7.5 million jobs in North America alone, leaving some 85 million "out of the workforce." EU (European Union) countries have added some 23 million to the same ranks, and Asia and the Middle East have piled on tens of millions more. The totals you reach on any particular day depend on your source and the definitions used, but let's turn data into usable information.

If you're not working, you're not spending; if you are afraid of losing your job, you are afraid of spending. Consumers (and companies) hunker down and hold back when uncertain of income. Unlike public sector strategies of spending as a way out, in private we get careful when money gets tight. How about the other half of the equation: capacity? This rightsizing of the job force is all about managing the balance of capacity and current demand, and if headlines are any indicator, we're not done yet. Companies and countries are still paring back. The United Kingdom is asking citizens to begin to pay more for health care, and industrial capacity utilization is at one of its lowest levels ever. Although we have excess capacity, we won't be rehiring. Not only have we rightsized the labor pool, we are still bringing pressure to bear to get better, faster, and cheaper as we do it.

But becoming more efficient is a good thing, right? Not for jobs. First, employers will add hours before head count every time. For decades, it was felt that unions had the upper hand, and as workweeks contracted, the workforce grew. Now the trend has reversed: People are working more hours, not fewer. Second—and this is a big one—according to some studies, if we get only 1 percent faster, that's 1.5 million jobs that won't come back . . . ever. No matter how you look at it, the math is working against us. If we lose 20 percent of any given labor pool and gain back 20 percent, we're still down. Think about it: Lose 20 percent, we need a 25 percent gain to get even; lose 50 percent, it takes 100 percent growth just to get back to where we started.

Let's finish this economic tour by considering some real-world examples and convert information into effect. Median family incomes are dropping; some are lower than they were 10 years ago. Ask around; most likely four out of five professionals will tell you they are worse off than they were 18 months ago. Private sector payrolls are also lower than they were 10 years ago, and with the government load (taxes), it now costs $84,000 to pay someone $50,000 plus $14,000 in benefits (do the math—it's really working against us). Look around. There are many, many other visceral signs of economic shift: those taking early Social Security retirement, the number of children living with grandparents (1 in 10), the numbers on some form of government assistance, and even the numbers of wedding rings for sale on Craigslist and the increase in individuals divorcing yet still living with their exes (we're not kidding, the data is out there).

Will those jobs come back? It's hard to tell. In the areas of real estate and finance, it is doubtful. Health care most likely will be very resilient with the aging of populations in Western countries. Retail and leisure occupations? Who knows? That will depend on disposable income. Automotive and manufacturing? Those jobs are expected to drop significantly over the next five years (do you know it takes only 24 hours of labor to build most cars today?). We do know that many of us currently work in jobs that 30 years ago weren't even listed as occupations by the U.S. Census Bureau. We'll see what tomorrow brings—only hindsight is 20–20—but let's shift our focus from economic effect to organizational response.

ORGANIZATIONAL RESPONSE

What's an organization to do? How have most responded to the challenge of keeping their salespeople effective in a marketplace gone mad? Unfortunately, the typical response has been an attempt to engineer the human being out of the equation. We know you can think of countless examples of companies that now try to manage the customer-company interface technologically rather than biologically. Instead of providing interaction with a living, breathing human being, many organizations now entice you (and some even force you) to enter your own data, print your own documentation, check in at automated stations or over the Internet, transfer funds electronically, "send away" for credits, buy through assigned customer advocates who have their own "mandates" from their boss, or spend an eternity in automated phone hell—all in the name of some twisted definition of "serving you better." Organizations are betting that if they can remove human unpredictability and inconsistency from customer interactions, we will all be happier and healthier (and cheaper to deal with, of course). The watchword seems to be "if you have the right process, interaction doesn't matter."

What's wrong with this picture? Where does this story hurt? We can tell you from having asked thousands of sales and service workshop participants to chart the satisfying and dissatisfying moments they've experienced as customers that in 9 out of 10 cases the satisfying or dissatisfying variable was the person with whom they interacted. Whether recounting a surgical procedure, buying a car, or taking part in a business-to-business sale, they never speak of the surgeon's technique—it is the bedside manner that left them happy or unhappy. It wasn't the vehicle that "surprised and delighted" them, it was the caring of the consultant. It wasn't a drug's ingredients that engendered repeat business, it was the human interface with the pharma rep. Interpersonal interaction, though sometimes not the top reason for making a purchase is almost always the reason for not repurchasing. The human asset (you) will make or break the purchase and ownership experience for a customer: That is what some organizations seem to forget.

What is that worth? What value can be placed on the human asset? We seem to quantify everything else under the sun; why not the caring, commitment, and understanding of those who work for us? There are three commonly used methods to estimate the value of any workforce: cost-based, market-based, and income-based. In a cost-based calculation, we can look at payroll to see what someone "costs" the organization in terms of pay and benefits. People's value is what they cost us. In the second method, we can take the same approach but look outside the organization to see what someone is worth to others—what that person's "market value" is. Through wage and compensation reports we can see what other companies pay their people. The third method involves estimating how much income an employee brings in. This can be done easily for salespeople (we do it every day, week, or month), and for others the average "revenue per employee" can be determined by dividing annual revenue by the total number of employees.

Do any of these methods provide an overall value of the workforce—the value of the human asset of any specific organization? We don't think so. Extending the thinking of Rensis Likert, a well-known organizational psychologist, we would like to submit a forgotten method of calculation we call replacement-based valuation. Simply put, what would it cost to replace the staff—or to establish it in the first place? If an organization had all the real estate and equipment in place but no one there, how long would it take and what would it cost to get the enterprise up and running at 100 percent? Somewhere between two and three times the current annual payroll seems to be a consensus for the asset value of a workforce. A friend of ours owns a small printing and fulfillment company that employs around 30 people. Annual payroll averages around $2 million, and so the value of the human asset would total some $5 million ($2 million times 2.5). This asset doesn't show up on the annual balance sheet like the building, the printing presses, or the company vehicles, but it is an asset: a $5 million asset that can appreciate or depreciate.

Income from asset liquidation is not earnings. We're going to say it again: Income from asset liquation is *not* earnings. If your senior management sells an asset, perhaps a building, and the money from that sale goes to the bottom line, is that truly earnings? Of course not. Using the same logic, if your organization continually squeezes you to gain additional efficiencies, leads through fear to gain output, and takes back pay and benefits to improve the bottom line, is that truly earnings? It certainly is not. Unfortunately, too many organizations are pulling a significant portion of their "earnings" from this liquidation of their human assets. Some have gotten away with it for several years, but sooner or later they will pay a price. We don't believe that anyone would disagree that a motivated, committed employee is a more valuable asset than one counting Sundays until retirement or awaiting the upturn that will allow him or her to leave a role as an economic hostage.

CUSTOMER VERSUS COMPANY

Let's add one final ingredient to the mix. Your job is only going to get harder (sorry about that) as a result of the expectations of those around you. Take a moment to think about the expectations of your customers or even your own expectations as a consumer. What's been happening to those expectations in recent years? Are they rising or falling? Do you expect and even demand more for your dollar than ever before? We suggest that customer expectations have gone up for a number of reasons:

- **Information.** Customers today come to the interaction armed with more information than ever. In fact, today's customer is far better educated about your product or service, with new data sources appearing every day. Blame Google if you need to, but the salesperson isn't the horse's mouth anymore.
- **Options.** Customers have a much broader competitive selection from which to choose; perhaps it's the perceived commoditization of so many industries. The half-life of a product or service monopoly today is brutally short.
- **Amenities.** With so many suppliers competing for business—and offering enticements to attract you to switch—customers have come to expect a certain "worth" or equity to their patronage, and they want it up front.

Now let's add the second horn of the expectations dilemma: *organizational expectations.* What is happening to what organizations are willing (or able) to do for their existing customer base? Think about what your organization is offering in terms of its baseline product or service. Is this level going up or down in today's economy? Are companies providing more amenities and autonomy or less in serving the customer? We think you'll find countless industries dropping their levels of baseline offerings:

- When was the last time you were served a meal on a flight or received a follow-up call on a large purchase?
- What is happening to return and refund policies at retail? Are they becoming more liberal or more restrictive?
- Do the reps at your local bank now demand two pieces of identification even though you've known them for years?
- Does your organization now add separate charges for freight or other line items that might have been included in the past?
- Are communications between you as a consumer and those you buy from improving or deteriorating (don't you love being on hold and being told that the reason for the wait is "unusually high call volumes" instead of the real reason—their staffing decisions)?
- At the simplest level, do you find yourself more or less satisfied these days with the responsiveness of the organizations with which you come into contact? Research resoundingly says less satisfied, *much* less.

THE CHALLENGE AHEAD

In closing this chapter, let's bring it home to you. The impact of all that we've discussed so far takes a real toll on your world, adding to the tough balancing act you manage every day in the world of the sales or service professional:

- There is a crying need to generate new accounts, yet lead generation is tougher than ever.
- Sales quotas are rising far faster than compensation.
- Restricted client budgets mean more competition for smaller amounts of money, with more and more stakeholders involved in the decision making.
- Cross-selling and the up-sell are profitable (U.S. airlines made $8 billion, or 6 percent of their revenues, from sales other than tickets, such

as seat upgrades, meals, and luggage), but it's often a very sore spot in customer research.

■ Although we traditionally focused on the alignment of sales and marketing, today our problems more often result from a lack of alignment between sales and *service*. Moving service providers into sales has evolved, as one client put it, "from afterthought to overkill" almost overnight.

■ The pace of customer response is accelerating, yet salesperson ramp-up is longer, more costly, and more difficult than ever. An average of 23 people are interviewed to arrive at a single hire, costing us upward of $100,000 to get to a productive rep. This is expensive for the organization and often painful for the customer counting on that salesperson.

■ Quotas and targets are rising to make back what we've lost, yet we've experienced a huge drop in those meeting quotas (less than 60 percent) and organizations making plans (less than 80 percent).

■ With fewer deals available, we know we need to close more of the ones we go after, yet we see across-the-board declines in the percentage of leads resulting in meetings, meetings resulting in presentations, and presentations resulting in sales.

■ Finally, we know that our business is more competitive and that our customers define value rationally and emotionally and know that the sales conversation is moving up in complexity and even organizationally, yet we also know that personal effectiveness in sales personnel is dropping, with less than 25 percent of salespersons being proficient in core selling skills competencies.

So what do we know to be true at this point? Like it or not, the role of the sales professional will be the fulcrum, or balance point, between rising customer expectations and falling service levels. *You* will live the daily struggle to integrate company and customer needs. We believe that you have the toughest job in the world, where strategy meets execution and intent meets reality. The game *has* changed again, and there is no rule book.

Our collective premise is that many of the habits that have brought you this far will no longer serve. The game has changed irretrievably; the stock answers of 1987 or even 2007 don't apply. As you map out a plan for where you want to be professionally or personally over the next few years, understand that what got you here won't get you there, but know too that we will give you the key to what will get you there—to both increased sales and improved relationships.

So What . . . Now What: The Art of Reflection

More than 200,000 texts are sent every second, and more than 100 trillion e-mails went across our collective desk last year. How many of them showed up in your in-box? How often were you tagged every day?

We know we're losing the capacity to connect with others (more about that in Chapter 4), and with so much information hitting us every day, we're losing the ability to connect even with ourselves. We're losing the capacity for reflection, for learning from the information we receive. Perhaps two very simple questions can force a moment of reflection:

1. *So What?* As you finish each chapter of this book, ask yourself: So what? What makes it meaningful, and why does it matter to me? This allows you to analyze and evaluate.
2. *Now What?* This second query—Now what? What should I do with this information?—is about integrating what we've written into what you do.

In closing each chapter we will offer thought starters for you, but it is your reflection on So What?/Now What? that can transform our ideas into your behaviors.

Two Worlds Collide: Functional versus Human

2

A few years ago some of us were lucky enough to spend the day with several hundred Ohio University students as part of their Sales Centre, a two-year program of study offering a certification in sales. OU students can earn this certificate along with a bachelor's degree regardless of their major. We shared eight hours with Jeffrey Gitomer for a day of networking and development in sales techniques and principles and believe without reservation that those students were the most composed and articulate young adults we've met before or since. Here was a group from several departments (from English to engineering to economics) working through the Centre's curriculum—every one of them sought after, polished, and prepared for success in whatever they do as members of the millennial generation.

There is another, very personal stake for us in this chapter on human skills in that we have nine children among us, from late teens to early thirties, and a generation of grandchildren already emerging. What we would like to do is leave our young adults and all those like them this lasting legacy of truth: The development of your human skills will provide you with a return far beyond any other because all of you, with very few exceptions, will find yourself in sales. That's right, *sales*. Even those of you who don't find "sales" in your title, particularly highly specialized engineers and technicians, will start out as "customer service engineers" or in customer support, with lots of regular customer contact on the horizon. Even if you have no direct customer contact, you'll be selling your ideas, your preferences, and your recommendations; you'll be selling *you* from day one.

How pervasive is the idea that everyone is in sales? The youngest of our collective brood of nine happens to be a very serious soccer player. At an Olympic Development Program meeting the presenter was a former university coach, professional player, and club director. He asked the audience of players and parents what they thought coaches look for most in a Division I soccer recruit. The responses included technical skills, tactical awareness, and conditioning, as you would expect, until the presenter silenced everyone with this statement: "We look for young adults who have the human skills to sell us on themselves." Unfortunately, many today in that age group would rather text their friends across the room than get up and talk to them. As a result, perhaps they are losing the capacity to interact and influence.

Is it any wonder, then, that many remain confused about selling—what it means and what it really involves? We aren't calling out only millennials. There are lots of people who started out elsewhere, from health care to engineering, who now find themselves responsible for revenue. We find that many, if they think about it at all, equate selling with a job that involves a commission. Particularly when considering the game-changing dynamics discussed in Chapter 1, there is a great deal of confusion around selling and what it involves.

THE ANATOMY OF SELLING

Allow us to offer some clarity about the structure of selling and what is involved regardless of the setting.

First, no matter who employs you or what your organization is selling or servicing, you work within two areas of responsibility; there are always two sides to your job: *functional* and *human.*

The Functional Side of Selling

The functional arena in any position involves the mastery of a product or service: knowing what you represent to your customer. This isn't a surprise to anyone; it's a given that you as a professional need to know the features, benefits, advantages, and proofs of what your organization does. This ownership of a product or service also

> **Functional: stressing purpose, practice, and utility**

can include a broader knowledge of your industry as well as competitive intelligence—knowing your customers and their needs and what *their* business and industry is all about.

To carry out your role on this functional side, you have to understand your organization's procedures, policies, process, and pricing. In other words, you need to be an expert in what it takes for someone to do business with you. If you were to complete a competency listing for insurance sales agents, you would find that besides having to know their products in auto, fire, property, marine, dental, medical, life, farm, malpractice, and who knows what other kinds of insurance, they have to know how to use computers, fax machines, printers, personal digital assistants (PDA), and software utilities covering everything from customer relationship management (CRM), enterprise resource planning (ERP), word processing, and spreadsheets to financial and other analytic programs.

All this and more without a single customer interaction. What are the functional requirements of your job? In other words, what do you have to be able to do just to earn the right to speak to the customer? Guess what: This functional arena alone won't be enough for you to be successful. Why? Because in so many industries there's not much differentiation of product or service, and there's probably more supply than demand in almost all businesses. In truth, functional excellence is only the ante that gets you into the game. It won't win it for you—*it won't get you there.*

The Human Side of Selling

The human arena is where you will win, keep, or lose a customer. On average, companies naturally turn over 10 percent of their customer base every year;

replacing that 10 percent and adding to it is the base challenge, and the human arena is where it happens. This assertion tends to create tension in some of us in that so many people have such conflict-ing ideas about what the human side of selling entails. People often assume that

> **Human: made up of people**

the human side of sales is something false and dishonest, something uncomfort-able (at least to the customer), and think that functional abilities ought to win it all for them (wishful thinking).

What is known is that it is the interaction between sales professional and customer that drives repurchase patterns and loyalty measures. You know it; you've lived it! Let's simplify the human side: Your interactions with custom-ers, regardless of what you sell, involve the combination of providing informa-tion and ensuring investment.

When you provide information, you educate the customer. You need to provide enough information, guidance, and direction so that the customer can do business with you effectively. You are responsible for educating your customers and prospects on how to do business with your organization.

By ensuring investment, you are making yourself accountable for your customers giving intangibly of *their* time, disclosing *their* information, and including your organization in

> **Invest: to spend time, money, or effort in exchange for future advantage or benefit**

their affairs. The endgame of the investment equation includes your customer investing tangibly in the form of budget dollars with you.

READINESS TO BUY

In effectively providing information and ensuring investment, you create and nurture readiness to buy: This is the by-product of the human arena. It is with this arena that we concern ourselves. Your functional arena is not our business—not even call planning, funnel management, and account strategy—we won't help you with that. However, we are expert in the applied behavioral sciences.

Simply put, we are masters of what makes people connect and disconnect. Disconnect, and customers go elsewhere; connect, create readiness to buy, and revenue happens.

So What? What did you learn?

- We are all in sales
- The anatomy of selling—functional and human
- Functional: mastery of feature, benefit, advantage, policy, pricing, procedure, and practice
- Human: providing information and ensuring investment
- Information: educating the customer
- Investment: intangible and tangible outcomes

Now What? What might you do now?

- Gather team members or others whose opinions you value to brainstorm the "subjects" where you are responsible to educate and then get a good description of who your end customers are.
- With the same group, list the most common intangible (time, disclosure) and tangible (decisions, approvals) outcomes you go for every day.

Creating Readiness to Buy: The State of the Moment

3

If the human side of your job is to create—that is, to bring about, to give rise to, to develop *readiness to buy*—we'd better understand what it is.

Buying readiness, simply put, is a product of *information* and *investment*. We said in Chapter 2 that your responsibilities in the human arena of selling involve providing information and ensuring investment. It's only fair, then, that the criteria you use to understand someone's buying readiness involve a subset of those variables.

Ready: prepared for action

Prospects' or customers' readiness to buy is affected by how informed they are and how invested they are in you as the salesperson, your organization, or the product or service you provide. With one of us having grown up in southeastern Michigan, it is easy to turn to the automobile industry as an example. One customer may be very informed and invested in driving only a four-wheel-drive vehicle for the Great Lakes winters. In that case, the customer's readiness is very high for a particular type of product. Another customer may be very ready only in reference to buying a particular brand, perhaps a Ford, because his parents worked their whole lives for that company. Yet another customer may be highly invested and experienced with her sales representative and would follow that rep to whichever dealership he went to regardless of the brand of car he sells. This customer's loyalty is not to the product but to the salesperson. In general, readiness to buy can be based on loyalty to one of many variables or a combination of them and can change very quickly—it's a moving target.

In a business-to-business context, we have had the honor of working with the Ford Motor Company for over 20 years. Our original client, Dean Coffman, used to go to lunch with us, and while we discussed specifications and budgets for a new contract, he would take notes the entire time. At the end of the meal Dean would tear off his notes, hand them over, and say, "Give me that as a quote and it's done!" These were often six-figure contracts covering multiple years, and in our minds Dean was about as high in readiness to buy as one can get. He had a track record of spending with us over 15 years; he allocated significant budgets, committing each time for a long period; and he even wrote our quotes for us. His loyalty to our organization, product, brand, and people set a benchmark few could hope to reach.

What about the other end of the spectrum? What about people with very *low* levels of readiness to buy? Actually, the next example shows both ends of the spectrum within the same person. One of the world's largest brewers is a longtime customer of our sales training approaches for that company and its wholesale employees. They love our sales development programs, our people, and the results we've delivered over the years. But the client, whom we'll call Bob, won't even consider our leadership offerings. Why? How could someone be so ready to buy one product but not another? In this case, the client organization has its own homegrown leadership training program. Any other management development offering is viewed as redundant or irrelevant to that curriculum. Bob's readiness to buy our leadership products or services (for now, anyway) happens to be pegged solidly at the low end.

What about *your* examples? What about your own clients? What are they very ready to buy? What are they not so ready to buy? Take a few minutes before reading further to think about your readiness to buy as a consumer: What do you *really* need or want? How ready are you for the things you love, and what are the items for which you have no readiness to buy, those you couldn't care less about? Take a thinking break for a moment and then let's look back over the years at how different schools of thought have approached the challenge of creating readiness to buy.

THE FIVE SCHOOLS OF SALES

If you Google "sales training"—within 14 one-hundredths of a second you will find 31,200,000 hits. A lot has been thought up, written, published, produced, and marketed over the years about how to develop the ever-elusive readiness to buy. We would like to organize this 70-year development of thought into five basic schools: relationship selling, steps to the sale, negotiation, strategic selling, and diagnostic approaches. Today's sales professionals can and still do utilize any one of these approaches to creating readiness—they all have validity. We feel no need to discredit any particular take on sales development, yet each one has evolved into the next in response to business conditions. We believe you'll agree with our conclusions on where it's going next.

Relationship Selling

Most sources credit the first phase in the formalization of sales development to the publication of Dale Carnegie's *How to Win Friends and Influence People* in 1937. Under the banners of ways to make people "like" you or "win" them to your way of thinking or even to "change" people without giving offense, Carnegie began it all and put the *relationship-centered approach* in motion. This approach entails creating rapport with others to get them to think, feel, or do something you want and feel good about it.

Steps to the Sale

The next organized effort toward sales effectiveness was born of the desire to replicate what successful salespeople do. The thinking was that if we can't get our salespeople to be more like those leading the board, let's get them to copy what successful sellers do—copy their process if you will. An era of initials was born. In the 1950s the first sales training acronym came out: AIDA, standing for "attention, interest, desire, and action." In essence, AIDA was meant to depict what we as customers go through when we buy something: First something gets our *attention;* maybe it sparks our *interest;* with luck and a little relevance we *desire* it; and finally we take *action* to buy it. Attempts were made at the same time to establish a normative set of five, six, or seven steps to the sale that the salesperson should go through every time to cover every one of the phases of buying.

Negotiation

Following these efforts to engineer the interpersonal process between customer and salesperson, there evolved a sales approach centered much less on the players in the drama and more on the transaction itself: *Negotiation* took over. Now the sale was viewed in terms of power and information: analyzing your own position as well as that of your opposition—your customer. Although it includes win-win tactics as well, negotiation centers on the deal: the transaction taking place between and among parties.

Strategic Selling

The next paradigm in developing sales professionals came about in the 1980s and 1990s and centered on the idea of each sale taking place within the context of delivering measurable *strategic* improvement to the customers' businesses as well as the salesperson's business. It wasn't enough to address a problem anymore; in a strategic approach a salesperson has to address the problem along with its underlying causes and propose a comprehensive solution. Demonstrating one's solution's connection to a bigger picture is the hallmark of the strategic approach. This inclusion of the higher-level "why of the buy" raised the bar and took place, we believe, in response to the economic changes of that era. It was a time of industry consolidation, shakeout, partnering, and acquisition; the bigger picture permeated everything we did.

Diagnostic Approaches

The final selling frame of reference is the *diagnostic* approach to effective influence. These "situational" influence models all involve first making a diagnosis of the customer's communication style, personality traits, or other behaviors to "match up" to the customer. DISC, Social Styles, Neuro-Linguistic Programming, and Myers-Briggs are all good examples of the diagnostic approach to influence effectiveness.

TIME

As we just said, all these approaches have merit and power in developing readiness to buy. They also all had their genesis in the business dynamics of their day. What about our day? We believe that the business climate today is different. We believe that the dynamics of buying and selling in the second decade of the new millennium demand a *new* paradigm, a *new* frame of reference, and a *new* way to understand and maintain readiness to buy.

Let's take a pause to orient ourselves. Over these first three chapters we've continually sharpened the focus, starting with a macro-level economic perspective, then zooming in on the human arena, and now having a singular focus on the concept of creating and maintaining readiness to buy as the primary responsibility of any sales-related activity. So what is different about today? What is it about human interactions in selling today that is any different than it was 10, 20, or 50 years ago? In a word, time.

There was a wonderful presentation given by David M. Levy, a professor at the University of Washington, called "No Time to Think." Professor Levy's premise was that we are losing our capacity for deeper thought and reflection because of the pace of working and living in the twenty-first century. We would like to take a giant leap forward and suggest that we are losing our capacity not only for reflection but for connection. Far more critical to the world of sales is the idea that *there is no time to be.*

We find that our collective concept of time is accelerating and fragmenting to the point where, if we let it, the functional will crowd out the human. In the name of productivity and efficiency, the very technology that is supposed to free us will enslave us—perhaps it already has.

TECHNOLOGY

Consider 24/7, 365, real-time, fast-time, more time, save time, better, quicker, cheaper, e-mail, cell phone, voice mail, texting, Facebook, Twitter, Google,

Skype, online blogging, surfing, ordering, dating, matchmaking—we aren't alive without them. Brand names become verbs overnight, and we find in our work that very few of us ever turn it off. Nineteen out of twenty confess to never using the power button on their cell phones. How about you? From purchase to replacement without ever powering down, we're so afraid of losing touch or missing out on new technology that we lose touch with ourselves and with others.

These timesavers then become time *takers.* Can you start or end your day without your fix of social networking or e-mail sorting, gathering or disseminating online news and humor? How much of it is fit to print? How much of it is worth the review? Do you find yourself disappointed and disillusioned daily with the process? Many do. How do we cope? What is our collective response when the urgent clouds the important? How about "5-hour Energy" when coffee or cola isn't quick enough or strong enough? How about a DVR so we can fast-forward through our televised entertainment more efficiently?

THE STATE OF THE MOMENT: BEING PRESENT

Do you find yourself all too often on autopilot? Do you forget names immediately on a first meeting? Does it take extraordinary amounts of time to recognize physical tension in your body? Do you move in a rush from one task to the next? Do you experience a variety of emotions without conscious realization? Do you break or spill items on a regular basis without knowing why?

These are all signs of difficulty *being present*—the state of being aware of and attentive to what is taking place in the moment.

Do you know that on a scale of 1 to 6, with 6 representing the greatest degree of being present, most people average around 3.5 when it comes to this skill of intentional consciousness? And it is a skill—one that can be sharpened or dulled by a variety of factors. It is a skill that pays dividends, both personal and professional. In our personal lives the capacity to be present is strongly correlated with lower levels of self-absorption, depression, anger, anxiety, hostility, and impulsiveness and higher levels of happiness and well-being.

For professionals, there is a direct relationship between being able to reside in the moment—while with others—and self-regulation. By always being present in our professional lives, we foster the ability to manage destructive interpersonal urges such as interrupting and ignoring others. Perhaps most important to a salesperson, the ability to be present is also directly related to the skills of emo-

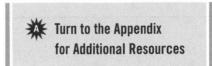

A Turn to the Appendix for Additional Resources

tional intelligence and even some aspects of social desirability. Selling today is no longer about the state of the relationship. Think instead, what is the state of the moment?

The state of the moment in sales involves developing a competency for being present with your prospects and customers, acting on purpose in real time with those who are important to you. Welcome to a new era in sales and selling.

So What? What did you learn?

- Your job: creating readiness to buy
- The schools of selling: relationship, steps, negotiation, strategic, diagnostic
- Fighting time and technology
- The new school; the state of the moment

Now What? What might you do now?

- Go to Appendix A and complete the Mindful Attention Awareness Scale (MAAS). The MAAS is a 15-item questionnaire designed to assess a core characteristic of dispositional mindfulness—namely, open awareness of and attention to what is taking place in the moment. See how present you are on a regular basis.

An Era of Empathy: The X Factor in Sales

4

The focus of our efforts is to help you maintain and leverage a hardwired *connection* with those who matter to you. Direct identification with another person's situation, feelings, and motives *is what will get you there*. The belief that you understand and acknowledge a person—that you not only viscerally understand but *care* about that person within the context of your business interaction—already exists almost without your trying. Let's explore the magic of empathy, the balance of empathy and ego in sales, the science of empathy, and what it means today in building your book of business.

To understand empathy, think about what happens to you when you watch a heavy hit during a hockey game. How do you react—emotionally and even physiologically—when you channel surf and catch a mixed martial arts cage match or a blooper reel of skateboarders landing face first on the concrete? Do you cringe? Does your pulse quicken

> **Empathy: the action of understanding, being aware of or sensitive to, and even vicariously experiencing the feelings, thoughts, and experience of another.**

and your blood pressure rise? Do your muscles flex and tense up, and in some instances do you react so strongly that you have to shift position, stand up, remember to breathe, change the channel, or turn the television off?

We're betting this is the case. This is empathy at its most raw. This is what we mean by understanding and being sensitive to the feelings, thoughts, and experiences of another person. This *action* (and it is an action) of connecting with another human being is empathy. And it's not just brutality and another's pain that we connect to. Can you recall the scene in *Forrest Gump* in which Tom Hanks is standing over Jenny's grave, updating her on how "little Forrest" is doing? Can you recall the lump in your throat by the end of that conversation? That too is empathy in action. Though we know that Forest is only a movie character and that it makes no difference to the Detroit Red Wings whether we connect with them while watching a hockey game, it *does* make a difference to your customers that you connect and stay connected.

What do we know about empathy? From the evidence of several fields of scientific study we know that humans are essentially *social* animals; just about everything we do is either in reaction to another or targeted to others, and it starts early. Day-old newborns are known to start crying at the sound of another baby's distress. Within the first months of life (some studies show in the range of 12 to 21 days) they begin to mimic the expressions of others as a connecting mechanism—it's hardwired. Not only can they reflect the tone and sentiment of an expression (such as happiness or sadness), babies can specifically mimic the expressions you use, whether it's sticking your tongue out or opening your mouth wide in surprise. This simple mimicry is the genesis of more complex connections, and by somewhere around two years of age people start to react with helping gestures in response to the distress of others.

What is taking place within us that we connect so naturally and organically with one another? It begins with mirror neurons within the brain that "couple," or integrate, the pathways carrying both perception and action. Perception-action coupling takes place on the same neural network that carries the information for both observation and execution. In other words, the same wiring is used. We like the analogy of the local cable service. A single cable comes into your house carrying the signals for television, Internet, and telephone. With most providers, while you are watching a television program a notification comes up on the screen to let you know that a phone call is coming in, what the number of the caller is, and the name that is associated with the number. These shared pathways within the brain also use the same wiring to carry information about an action we observe or perceive, along with information associated with an action we perform.

Guess what: These are *two-way* connections. At the simplest level, even babies recognize when someone is imitating them. Two bodies are connected regardless of who is executing and who is observing. At higher levels, this mirroring literally maps the feelings of others onto one's own nervous system—feelings of pleasure *or* pain. By using functional magnetic resonance imaging to map two brains that are either viewing or experiencing pain, it's possible to literally see the overlap, the common path. This capacity for vicarious pain is also well documented as a predictor of higher forms of empathy—not just feeling another's pain but experiencing the urge to mitigate the pain even though it is someone else who is suffering.

Where do we take this knowledge? That is the paradox. We know that we naturally connect with others both emotionally and physiologically and usually do so without trying. So what do we do with it? We know this sense of a shared right-brain experience is a prerequisite to understanding what drives another person's intentions and motivations, leading to effective social interaction. So now what? What do we do to convert knowledge into a positive effect in sales for you? We engage empathy to balance ego.

Across any study of what it takes to make it in sales, a powerful ego generally tops the list. The intrinsic need to persuade and convince someone else—along with the resilience of ego to take the battering of rejection—has been a cornerstone trait in selling for as long as we've studied it. This, admittedly, is what got us "here" in sales. Yet as we've already discussed, it is different today. What got us here will not get us to the next level by itself. Ego alone is failing us in sales—it is killing us. You've seen it; you've experienced it. Adding the need to connect to the need to persuade in sales will get us to the next level, and the conscious maintenance of empathy in sales simply involves convincingly communicating that you understand your customers' perspective and that you care. A prospect believing that you understand and you care will get you there; the balance of ego and empathy makes that possible.

Still need proof? Consider your role as a consumer of goods and services. On average, do you feel that the organizations you do business with care about and connect with you? Your phone carrier, utilities supplier, insurance provider, car dealer, banker or accountant, and business-to-business partners—do you believe they understand and care? For the majority of you the answer today is no. Ego is still in the way; the salesperson's ego overrides your needs. We also overwhelmingly find that if and when you do believe that someone has made a connection with you and understands your place in the buying process, you will stay with that person, switch to that person, and bring others with you.

Empathy balancing ego—*this* is what will get you there. It will get you to sales success and effectiveness as well as to where you want to be personally and professionally. In Chapter 5 we will provide a brand-new perspective for maintaining the natural empathic connection built on the idea that sometimes the easiest path to growth is simply not going backward.

So What? What did you learn?

- Empathy: the action of understanding the feelings, thoughts, and experiences of others
- Empathy: wired from birth to care
- Empathy balancing ego—that will get us there

Now What? What might you do now?

- Estimate your empathy-ego quotient; divide a pie chart on paper into your empathy-ego balance.
- Watch a hockey game and notice your physiological reactions.
- Rent and watch *Forrest Gump* for the same reason, especially near the end when Forrest talks to Jenny at her graveside. How do you respond?

A New Approach to Change: Easier to Stop Than Start

5

We hope that everything we've put forward up to this point has been logical as well as supported by and congruent with what you would hope for in a book such as this. However, most of you probably are expecting that now we will try to tell you what to do in the selling equation. You may be looking to read a set of competencies, skills, and steps for establishing an empathetic connection with your customers. Let's not do that. Let's leave that to other authors. What we want to do is tell you what *not* to do—how *not* to bankrupt the empathy-ego equation.

Peter Drucker, one of the finest thinkers of the twentieth century, was known for several key concepts related to personal change. Our favorite and a foundational principle for this book can be summed up by paraphrasing Dr. Drucker: We spend a lot of time teaching people what to do; we don't spend enough time teaching people what to stop doing. Many people don't need to learn what to do; they just need to learn what to stop doing.

Think again about your interactions as a consumer in which the salesperson or service provider left you wanting. In most cases there was an annoying interpersonal habit that put you off: talking on and on, checking his BlackBerry, ignoring you to take a phone call, keeping her eyes glued to the computer screen, conducting a side conversation with a coworker. What we find is that there are usually one or two interpersonal habits that if eliminated would make the difference between connect and disconnect, between empathy and apathy. We also find that the longer people work at the craft of selling, the more their errors are behavioral sins. When you have been at selling for a while, your problems won't come from a lack of product mastery or industry knowledge. They will come from issues that your behaviors create that can and should be fixed right now.

But what's the rush? We have saved one final dynamic of empathy from Chapter 4 that in our minds creates this sense of urgency: Empathy is eroding! People today are collectively losing their capacity to connect with one another. The Institute for Social Research at the University of Michigan has collected solid data in 72 major studies since 1979, polling over 14,000 college students. What have they found? These young adults are 40 percent less empathetic than they were in 1979; they are 40 percent less likely to describe themselves as having tender or concerned feelings for others. That shift took the form of a steep drop that began in 2000.

Empathy is down; narcissism is up. The very ability to think about how someone else might feel is declining. Adding insult to injury, the capacity to express a response to the distress of another person has dropped even more sharply. Both cognitive empathy and emotional empathy have crashed, and not just among college students. Further studies have shown that younger adults are losing this potential whether or not they have gone to college.

You might be asking; Why the relatively sudden, drastic crash in the empathy market? After all, it was stable for over 20 years before taking a steep dive. Our consensus would be that the culprit is the very technological advances we discussed earlier: The generation brought up with the Internet, instant messaging, cell phones, and computers is the one losing the capacity. Yet does it really matter *why* it has happened? We have a saying: "It is easier to get un–screwed up than it is to figure out how and why we got screwed up in the first place." Our focus here is on a powerful, proactive countermeasure.

We feel a sense of urgency in sales to reverse this trend, and this is what we offer: a simple approach to maximizing your role as fulcrum between customer expectation and corporate imperative. What we propose to you is simply reversing the two sides of a well-known coin. Whereas once common sense might have counseled you to "start paying more attention to customers," "stop talking about yourself so much" is now the watchword. We now frame behavioral change not in terms of perhaps "listen more attentively" but in terms of "stop playing with your BlackBerry while others are talking." Most of us are geared to acknowledging the doing of something rather than its absence.

The funny thing about stopping some behaviors in business is that it gets less attention but can be as crucial as anything else we can do. In our personal lives we often congratulate ourselves (and receive recognition from others) for what we successfully give up: smoking, certain foods (often our favorites), even watching too much television. But we often lose this common sense in the organizational environment, in which reward systems are solely based on what we've done, what numbers we've delivered this month, or what revenue growth we've posted.

We can change that. All that's required is a slight tweak in our mindset, in the way we look at behavior. Get out your notepad. Instead of your usual "to-do" list, start a "to-stop" list. Don't worry about stopping everything, just stopping *something*.

What follows is a surprisingly familiar compilation of what we know we all do at one time or another that turns off our customers, our friends, and even our loved ones. It is a list of what we unconsciously do to destroy instead of nurture the empathic connection: *what keeps us from reaching the next level in sales.*

So What? What did you learn?

- The empathy market crash of 2000
- Over time, our deficiencies become predominantly behavioral.
- "We spend a lot of time teaching people what to do; we don't spend enough time teaching people what to stop doing." —Peter Drucker
- The habits that disconnect us

Now What? What might you do now?

- Make a list—write it down: What are the behaviors that salespeople and service providers engage in that drive you crazy? What do they do in your presence that you wish they would stop doing?

The 16 Habits Your Customers Want You to Give Up

The interpersonal issues that destroy organic empathy . . . knowing how to choose what to change.

- Review the ineffective interpersonal habits that can chill or kill your sales career.
- Understand the impact of information and emotion in the context of why we pick up bad habits.
- Gather data about yourself in preparing to select which bad habit to give up for your customers.
- Choose what to stop doing when interacting with others.

The Habits That Can Hold You Back in Sales

6

As you begin to consider this unique behavioral approach to the process of change, keep in mind that most behaviors are not good or bad in and of themselves. They are *value-neutral*. Behaviors generally take on value only in regard to when they are used and how they are delivered.

SHIFTING INTO NEUTRAL

This shift to understanding the concept of neutral is key to our approach to change. Let's say you work with certain customer segments that might not characterize you as the nicest person around. Let's take it further and say that you decide you want to change that perception. You decide, "I need to be nicer; I'm tired of all the tension."

What Should You Do?

For most people, a behavior change like this is a pretty tough process, and it calls for a long list of positive actions. Think about it: You have to start complimenting people, saying "please" and "thank you," noticing and commenting on things you feel are important to them, perhaps listening to your customers more effectively and patiently, maybe addressing them with more respect, and paying more attention to manners and common courtesy.

In effect, you have to transform all the negative things you do at work into *positive actions.* That's asking the impossible of most people (the authors included); it seems to require something close to a complete personality make-over. In our experience, very few, if any, people can institute that many positive changes in their interpersonal actions all at once. They can handle one at a time, but a half dozen or more? Not likely.

Fortunately, there's a simpler way of achieving the goal of being nicer: All you have to do is stop being nasty. It doesn't require much. You don't have to think of new ways of being sweeter to people. You don't have to design a daily reminder to make over the essence of you. You don't even have to remember to say nice things and hand out compliments and tell the little lies that lubricate the wheels of social intercourse. All you have to do is . . . nothing.

When a customer offers a lame excuse in her complaint, don't argue (as you know you can)—say nothing.

When another customer challenges your company policy, don't debate—quietly consider his side and say nothing.

This is not a semantic game. The beauty of knowing just which behavior to stop—of shifting into neutral—is that it is so simple to do.

Given the choice between becoming a nicer person and ceasing to be mean, which do you think is easier to do? One requires a concerted series of positive acts of *co*mmission. The other is nothing more than an act of *o*mission, of *not* doing.

Keep that in mind as you go through the list of interpersonal habits in this chapter and determine whether any apply to you. Correcting the behavior, you'll discover, does not require polished skills, elaborate training, arduous practice, or superhuman creativity. All that's required is the smallest bit of guts to stop doing what you've done in the past, in effect to do nothing at all.

Again, What's Wrong with Us?

Before we can talk about fixing faulty behavior, we must identify the most common flaws in the behavior of people in sales. We have done so, yet we hasten to add that these are a very specific breed of flaws:

- These are not flaws of skill, nor are they flaws in your knowledge of your industry, your customers, and your competition.
- These are not flaws in intelligence; some of the most brilliant people in the world have them.
- These are not flaws of unchangeable personality. Introvert, extrovert, right-brained, left-brained—we all have them.
- This is not a religious conversion. We're preaching to the choir in that we all know that rudeness can cost us plenty.

What we offer you now are challenges in interpersonal behavior: how we act with and toward others. They are the common, obvious, everyday annoyances that make our workplace and our customer relations substantially less pleasant than they ought to be. They are interpersonal behavioral habits that turn our customers off and turn them away.

Here are the 16 habits we will be addressing:

Habit 1—Failure to Be Present	Habit 10—Withholding Passion and
Habit 2—Vocal Filler	Energy
Habit 3—Selling Past the Close	Habit 11—Explaining Failure
Habit 4—Selective Hearing	Habit 12—Never Having to Say You're
Habit 5—Contact without Purpose	Sorry
Habit 6—Curb Qualifying	Habit 13—Throwing Others under the Bus
Habit 7—Using Tension as a Tool	Habit 14—Propagandizing
Habit 8—One-Upping	Habit 15—Wasting Energy
Habit 9—Overfamiliarity	Habit 16—Obsessing over the Numbers

Before we move on to cover each habit individually, we'd like to remind you to keep a few things in mind:

- **People in sales are not bad people.** They're some of the finest, most professional individuals in the collective workforce.
- **Many of us, inside sales and out, simply hold ourselves back.** Most of us have a personal failing or two that we aren't aware of or that we know about but don't feel the need to change.
- **You probably will see yourself in one or more of the habits we present in the following pages.** Please hold off on selecting any to work on for now. Chapter 9 will provide some important guidelines to use in picking what to work on. Right now, just take in the habits. See them in others. See them in yourself.

Habit 1—Failure to Be Present

Repeated and annoying displays of behavior that indicate that we would rather be somewhere else, some*when* else, or with someone else.

Within our collective professional experience we find that people today consider themselves to be as busy as they have ever been in their lives. The vast majority of people we work with are being asked to do more with less and do it quicker and better than at any time within their personal memory. This seems to apply to personal arenas just as much as to professional. We feel we are being pulled in more directions than we can manage at work, at home, and, sadly, at play.

Often we can take a peek into the human soul by assessing what people do when they feel they are alone. One place that provides the illusion of privacy is behind the wheel of a car. For some reason we feel free to do just about anything while driving. What have you observed other drivers doing while they "multitask" on the road? The easy answers are talking on the phone, eating a snack (or a *meal*), smoking, texting, and e-mailing. How about shaving, putting on mascara, and flossing teeth—all while controlling a vehicle of significant mass traveling at 70 miles per hour in traffic?

We understand that the information age is an era of multitasking. Productivity tools abound to help us keep up and keep pace, but have you noticed that we don't even use the on/off buttons anymore? It is one thing to try to leverage personal efficiencies, yet what about the bleed over into *inter*personal efficiencies? Can we apply the same thinking in reference to multitasking when we *aren't* alone? The answer is that we do—and we shouldn't.

How do you feel when interacting with someone who constantly looks away to check her BlackBerry (do you do that)? How about a salesperson who takes a phone call on his cell or, even worse, a landline at his desk and puts you on hold while you're standing right in front of him? Have you sat face to face with a salesperson whose attention drifts off in noticing someone else passing by (either a coworker or, worse yet, a perhaps more profitable customer)? At home, who is guilty of failing to make eye contact (or any other acknowledg-

Finishing up one client meeting and almost late for another, Jack was feeling antsy. Although he was dealing with a longtime client, *this* meeting was already over. He was just waiting for the purchasing information from his client's administrative assistant. She had gone to get the purchase order number assigned and had been gone 5 or 10 minutes already. The meeting he needed to get to was at Florida Power & Light, and that deal could be worth upward of $400,000. Actually, he didn't even have to stay and wait for the number. He wished he had excused himself and called her for the PO later from the car.

Sarah, the administrative assistant, came back with the paperwork. Having known Jack for a fairly long time, she began to tell him about having been off work the previous week. She said she had been helping out her sister-in-law, as her brother was seriously ill. The company hadn't approved her personal time off, and she told him it was unpaid time she couldn't afford. It was very important to her, yet she twice noticed Jack glancing down at his watch. She stopped cold for a moment and stammered, "It's pretty obvious you aren't interested. I'm sorry for taking up your time, Jack; here's your PO." Sarah quickly left the room, visibly upset.

Jack knew what he had done and felt awful about it. His mind had already been on the next meeting—the next deal at Florida Power & Light—and as a consequence he had been rude and inconsiderate to Sarah. Two days later he personally apologized to her, knowing she probably could forgive but not soon forget. As a result, Jack didn't wear a watch for two years after that—he never missed it.

ment past a grunt) because her attention happens to rest on a 50-inch flat-screen across the room?

Failure to be present in any part of our lives is right up there with selective hearing as a premier *apathy* generator. Nothing kills empathy and rapport faster than blatantly ignoring the individual with whom we are interacting. It is rude, so why do we do it? Simply put, it is the interpersonal equivalent of jet lag. If you have ever traveled across five or more time zones, you've probably noticed the effects of being accustomed to one time zone and trying to function in another. Failure to be present is the manifestation of a similar lag. Regardless of where we are, there are really only three real time zones we can live in: the past, the present, and the future.

Interpersonal problems arise when two people, although interacting, reside in different zones. When a customer or prospect is present, directly interacting with us, right now, do we reside in the same moment? Are we actively listening to and responding to that person's expressed needs? Or are we thinking about what the boss said in the sales meeting this morning? Are we thinking about what this deal might mean in terms of next month's commission check? Are we concerned with missing an up that just came in or the next meeting on our calendar? In short, are we present?

Another author and personal friend of ours is Silva Goncalves, a Brazilian psychologist. His mantra is "90–9 and 1." His prescription for being present is to strive to mentally spend your life 90 percent tuned in to the present, being aware of and living right now, 9 percent planning for the future, and only 1 percent quickly learning from the past. It is when these proportions get out of balance that we become less productive and, for our purposes here, far less effective with others.

What time zone do *you* live in? There is no daylight savings in relating to others. There can be no multitasking in communicating interpersonally. When you are in front of a customer or, more important, in front of your friends or family, set the productivity tools and strategies aside. Be present, be aware of the time, and go for effective, not efficient. Go for making the most of *now.*

Habit 2—Vocal Filler

The overuse of unnecessary (and meaningless) verbal qualifiers.

This annoying apathy generator takes place when we can't control our repeated use of meaningless words and phrases such as "like," "um," "you know what I mean," and "sorta," along with countless others that you can nominate yourself. Although this habit usually takes root in one's youth, it lasts through adulthood in many cases. When you hear vocal filler words coming out of others, take the time to count them; you'll be amazed at how heavy the offense can be. While you're at it, count them in an ESPN pregame show or during celebrity interviews (we'd also suggest keeping track of the number of times a teenager uses "like" in one short conversation, but don't be surprised if you exceed all available fingers and toes). Then count them when you use them with your customers—catch *yourself.* The problem here isn't one of faulty listening but one of excessive talking.

In fact, this habit is a twofer. The second, perhaps even more offensive use of vocal filler is the repeated use of *negative* qualifiers such as "no," "but," and "however" (just a pretentious version of "but"). The annoying habit of starting sentences in this way—intended or not—will communicate that the listener knows nothing and the speaker knows all.

This is subtle but deadly. The salesperson patiently waits for the customer to articulate the objection. Then, when it is time to answer that objection, he begins with something like "I can understand, *but*" or "I see your point; *however.*" As seemingly harmless (and as common) as that habit seems to be, it doesn't work. Why? you ask.

Because before you even have a chance to state your case, you have alienated your customer. You have (one hopes unconsciously) shown a lack of respect. How do you react when you think someone has dismissed you? Your customer probably will respond the same way.

By way of illustration, when you call an airline or car rental company today, the odds are that you will talk to a computer (another example of taking the human being out of the customer-company interface). You will be forewarned that "to provide you better service . . . ," the initial collection

Marcy thought to herself: "That's three 'e-ssen-shoe-alees,' two 'I'm being perfectly honest with you,' and four 'no, you're rights.'" She had noticed that Chandra, the vice president from Wainright's, continually inserted the word "e-ssen-shoe-alee" into her part of the presentation. "I'm sure she means 'essentially,' but it keeps coming out 'e-ssen-*shoe*-alee'; there's nothing 'sen-shoe-al' about the proposal they're presenting."

She also noticed that Francisco, the director, prefaced every bullet point with some variation on "honesty": "I'm going to be honest with you," "to be honest," "I *am* being honest," "let's be honest," "in all honesty," "to be completely honest." Enough! What was she supposed to think during the occasional lapses when Francisco wasn't prefacing what he was saying with some reference to honesty—that he was lying?

Marcy was beginning to fidget. She had looked forward to Wainright's bid and thought it might be the front-runner, but her concentration was waning. She was wearing down. Now it was Raul who was distracting her. She was thinking, "Stop saying 'no, you're right.' It's nice that you agree with me, Raul, and I appreciate the enthusiasm, but why do you start every sentence with the word 'no'? It's driving me crazy!"

Marcy had effectively checked out. Wainright's went from front-runner to a distant third, and it had nothing to do with its service, reputation, product, or price. It had to do with meaningless verbal tics and crutches, the verbal equivalent of not being able to see the forest for the trees. Too much mortar and not enough bricks.

of information will be automated. You'll get to answer questions about your account number, destination, options, and so on. In the early days of voice recognition software, the challenge for businesses using computers for this purpose was that the computers had to be programmed with definitions for common words and phrases. The meaning of the words "but" and "however" presented a special dilemma for the programmers. They finally settled on the following definition for both words:

Disregard previous information.

At first blush this doesn't seem like a good working definition, but (look, we just used it) think about it. Try it a few times. It fits the meaning perfectly. When someone conversationally begins with "no," "but," or "however," it conveys the exact same message: "disregard previous information."

It is hard to imagine a less effective way to begin a conversation, and it doesn't have to have a purely negative context. Even when *agreeing* with others you'll hear the regular use of "no, you're right." When it's not important, we do it. When it's a critical negotiation, we tend to do it even more.

The important messages from this habit, which are applicable to all ineffective interpersonal habits, are the importance of acting on purpose (premeditating your behavior with your customers) and the simplicity of the solution we offer: *doing nothing,* simply *stopping* the offending behavior. Simple but not easy.

Habit 3—Selling Past the Close

The irresistible urge to verbalize and execute every possible step in the sales process.

The three of us are not much into shopping. We have no problem buying what we need, but unlike others in our households, we don't particularly enjoy the process. However, with six daughters and three wives among us, we've witnessed buying and shopping from almost every possible angle.

We've also studied the *selling* process for a very long time, and this habit of selling past the close (also known as adding too much value) is one of the most serious examples of customer abuse in that lots of people are ready to buy long before the salesperson is done wanting to sell.

Picture a sales presentation that is going well. We have the customer's attention. We've effectively presented features, benefits, and advantages. The customer's interest level rises. We can sense it by the questions asked, the body language, and the tone of the discussion. We ask for the order. The customer says yes. That should be it, another successful call ending in a sale, but something happens. After the customer says yes, we keep talking. We're out of body now. We can't help ourselves. Somehow we have to let the customers know about the features we hadn't discussed. They don't know enough to buy yet.

Whether fueled by nerves, pressure from the boss, commission fever, or plain absentmindedness or boredom, sales professionals often disconnect. They have the occasional ability to break a perfectly functional empathic connection by refusing to let the customer determine when the sale is over. Too often customers have gotten to the point of being ready to buy—or maybe they were born ready to buy—and just want to make the purchase and move on to another part of their life, only to find that the salesperson just can't help himself.

For example, when one is taking delivery of a new vehicle from one of the Big Three, their sales standards "demand" that the sales consultant walk the customer over and introduce the customer to the service department manager before delivering the keys. Although their market research may indicate that introducing a customer to the service manager can be an effective relationship builder, it's a relationship *killer* if the customer wants to be done buying. If you

Verghese Jacob sold "tone." He was working for a CLEC (competitive local exchange carrier), sort of an independent rep for telephone numbers and phone lines. It was totally business to business; the unique proposition behind selling "tone" was calling on businesses that carry several phone lines (doctors, dentists, lawyers, accountants) and delivering savings on their phone service expenses. Verghese usually could figure on saving a prospect an average of $17 per phone line per month. In most cases he was able to drop the per-line cost from an average of $65 to $48. Prospects that had 8 to 10 lines could count on an annual savings of anywhere from $1,600 to $2,000.

The owners and senior partners of those businesses loved the idea of a couple of thousand dollars dropping into their pockets every year, and they didn't have to give up their current phone numbers to do it. About the only thing that changed was where the bill came from. Verghese always felt that if he could get the right appointment, he could close the sale. As commissions were structured so that he got the entire first month's billing as an incentive, it could mean $400 to $500 to Verghese personally for every prospect he could convert. Not bad.

Verghese was finishing up a successful meeting with the managing partner of a decent-sized law firm and was filling out the paperwork to carry over 12 lines. That came to 12 times $48, or $576 in his pocket. It had been a great week, he had been recognized as the "Top Seller" the previous year, and it looked like this year was off to a great start too.

As they were completing the paperwork, Verghese was still thinking about his commission when he absently asked the managing partner, "You don't have a contract with anyone, do you?" Looking up, he saw the partner slowly set the order aside, turn to face him, and say, "Yes, I do. Is that a problem?"

It wasn't a problem. Verghese regularly converted existing contracts. It was a bit more paperwork for him but rarely an obstacle. It was a question he didn't have to ask—the response wouldn't have made a difference—yet in that moment he felt compelled to fill the silence. He told the partner this, told her not to worry; he knew the ins and outs, and rolling a current commitment was no big deal.

Too late.

> She pushed her chair back a foot or so, leaving the order on the table. She told Verghese she needed to think about it before signing. She wanted to talk to her current provider about early termination fees or penalties.
>
> He had lost the sale (he never got it back).

feel the need to provide one more advantage, articulate one more value statement, or introduce the customer to one more key member of the staff, check the customer's eyes for a heavy glaze. If he's done with the sale, let him buy.

Customers will never know (or care) about what they've missed, and they'll thank you for being considerate of their needs and letting them decide when it's time to buy.

Habit 4—Selective Hearing

The absence of active listening in the presence of a customer.

Arguably the most powerful empathy killer in interpersonal relations in any context, the inability to pay attention can tick off even the most forgiving human beings. It can turn you from front-runner to runner-up in no time flat.

In trying to understand and study the art and science of listening, the consensus seems to be that there are several levels at which people listen. All the studies start with some descriptor of blatantly ignoring someone and progress to some semblance of paying evaluative attention (listening only in order to be immediately ready to put in our own two cents) and sooner or later arrive at an *active* level of listening.

In most discussions of listening there is also usually a personality component offered up for consideration. The theory is that although we are socialized by our parents, our bosses, and other significant people in our lives, we are hardwired at birth to have a number of specific social tendencies. Some people are naturally organized and like to plan their work; others prefer to be spontaneous. Some people are logical; others go with their gut.

We've been asked, "Aren't some people just better listeners?" This question usually comes with the tale of "three children who live in the same house, same parents and even the same teachers growing up, where each child is completely different," leading the teller to ask, "Doesn't that *prove* it's all hardwired from birth?"

In a word, no.

With listening, we believe that the relevant question comes down to this: Is this a natural skill or an acquired competence? The answer: Listening is *not* a natural skill but an acquired skill. It is developed by nurture, not just by nature. Introverts are thought to have a more natural ability to listen and tend to think things through before they speak. Extroverts, in contrast, are talkers. They talk to think. The good news (especially since so many salespeople are extroverted) is that listening skills can be learned—they can be acquired.

More good news: As is true in the remedy for other ineffective interpersonal habits, being a better listener usually requires doing nothing more than

Well into the process of responding to a request for proposal and a quotation for high-level database management software, Michael's team was assembled at the client site for the third round of presentations. There were three others with Michael and six client personnel seated in the conference room. The room was equipped with a ceiling-mounted projector, but before they could set up the laptop for PowerPoint, the lead client vice president asked for a few moments.

"There have been some complications today on our end that have nothing to do with this project or your presentation. These complications, however, dictate that we finish early with this presentation round." The VP was very friendly but appeared hurried and maybe a bit distracted. "We don't want to put off this decision by rescheduling to a later date, but we would like to ask you to limit your time to a total of 45 minutes. We would suggest a 30-minute presentation, leaving us 15 minutes for question and answer. We'll give you five minutes to discuss any changes you'd like to make before we start. Rest assured that all three providers are being asked to limit their presentations in the same way."

Michael and his team went out in the hall for a few minutes and were unanimous in their decision to pull one segment of the PowerPoint file. After reassembling in the conference room and setting up, they presented for a flat 20 minutes and opened it up for 25 minutes of active question and answer. At the 45-minute mark Michael called the time and thanked the client VP and her team for considering them.

Out in the parking lot the team took a few minutes to debrief before heading out. They had pulled all but the introduction to the segment on their organization's history, capabilities, and testimonials. They knew they weren't the first choice in this bid but believed they wouldn't have been there at all if the client didn't already know a fair amount about them. They had hit their approach, product, and value hard and then opened it up as they had been asked. They felt good about their chances and went back to the office.

Back in the client's conference room, the team thought to be the front-runner for the business was given the same request for a presentation lasting 45 minutes, including at least 15 minutes of question and answer. They agreed, took a few minutes in the hallway to regroup, and came back in to set up. They began speaking at 3:00 p.m., and at 3:40 they finished their presentation and asked if there were any questions.

Silence greeted them. The vice president responded, "No, I think we've gotten all the information we need for today. Thank you for coming and for being so flexible."

The front-runners left the client's team to discuss all the presentations of the day.

The vice president went to her office and called Michael: "I wanted you to be the first to know that we have decided to partner with you and your team on this project." She called the other two teams the next morning to give them the bad news. The team that could have—*should* have—won the business couldn't believe their ears.

"What went wrong? Why did we lose the bid?"

The VP said, "You didn't listen."

nothing. Give seven seconds of silence a try. We're serious; do nothing. Try to allow seven seconds to go by without the customer hearing your voice during a meeting (you may not be able to at first).

The prescription simply dictates the *stopping* of something. When listening in a less than effective manner, we're most often engaged in all sorts of insulting behaviors from blathering, to arguing, to "topping," to expressing impatience all the way up to cutting people off and finishing their sentences for them (isn't it hard enough to finish our *own* sentences intelligently?). Curing interpersonal deafness is the single endeavor with the highest return and highest payout in which you can engage. Your customers will thank you, your loved ones will thank you, and you will feel proud of yourself.

Habit 5—Contact without Purpose

Repeated deliberate communication for no valid business reason (other than wanting to sell something).

"I'm just calling to touch base, see how you're doing." How many times have we heard that? How many times have we *said* that? We may be driven by a short-term sales push, a bad economy, a current promotional effort, or even a couple of empty hours that we feel a guilty need to fill. In any case, what does the customer hear? We're trying to put lots of sincerity into our voice in asking, "How *are* you?" and most likely all the customer hears is, "I have no real purpose to call that would matter to you, and I thought I would just stop by, show my face, and waste some of your time." What is in play here is a touch without purpose.

Since the beginning of the twentieth century, researchers have known that a multi-touch approach works. Marketing experts contend that it takes several touches (the consensus seems to be four to six) before people are ready to buy. In fact, we know that lead-to-sale ratios grow when several spread-out touches are used versus a single larger blast. The basic logic is that if you try to close on the first touch, that is too soon, just as when our kids push for an answer right now, the answer will be no. Conversely, if you're still making a closing attempt after 10 or 12 touches, give it up: The sale is *not* going to happen no matter how much you or your boss needs the revenue. Contact can be everything from phone calls to sending information or simple advertisements or marketing campaigns.

Let's add the multi-touch missing link: It has to be a *touch with a purpose.* In planning messages, contacts, calls, visits, or e-mails to your prospects, there has to be a valid reason to reach out. There has to be a viable need for the contact in the customers' eyes; it can be either a logical or an emotional anchor, but there *has* to be an anchor.

What is our message, then? If the "touch" only meets some pressing need *you* might have, don't do it. If the urge to reach out is just an itch you have in the moment, don't scratch it. A touch without purpose is an empathy killer. We connect with customers and prospects on myriad levels. It happens natu-

Andy, the president, sat alone, perplexed and dismayed. He had built a profitable organization over 20 years with seven locations, committed people, great products and services, and an enviable reputation in industrial supply. With everything seemingly moving in the right direction, what was up with this report?

He had commissioned a study surveying 200 of the company's customers. They were careful to hit every type of company, every region, and every product mix they could isolate. They queried the customers about satisfaction, process, pricing, and quality, and when the results came back, the number one customer complaint was, "We see your salespeople too often!"

How could that be? How can they see salespeople too often? Is that even possible? Andy looked into it first with the sales management staff. When asked about decision-making criteria for which customers were called on and when, the management group showed him that a great deal of thought had gone into route scheduling. Significant consideration was given to efficiency, timing, and purchase patterns; he didn't know where to fault their logic. Andy next went to the sales group, which reinforced sales management's picture of a planned, regular, consistent contact process that was based on the potential of each particular account.

Andy finally called some of the top customers and heard a very different story. "Yes, your people are here too often. We love you guys, but they aren't here for my needs, they are here for your needs. Sometimes we feel like we're just part of a milk run where you show up every Tuesday rain or shine; the problem is we don't need to see you every Tuesday. We have tried as politely as possible to suggest they come less often, but your people say their boss wants them here no matter what. Have you ever thought how annoying and disruptive it can be to our business every time they show up?"

Andy was floored. He had thought they were very customer-driven. He apologized and dedicated himself to letting customer needs drive contact in the future.

rally, it even happens spontaneously, and with experience in our respective businesses we know that the touches that carry purpose are the touches that *maintain* empathy. If we take the time—each and every time—to make sure the contact we're about to make has a purpose, we reward our customers. We reward ourselves.

Habit 6—Curb Qualifying

The tendency to judge a prospect's means and motive superficially from a distance.

This is a common practice across the retail and real estate sectors: Sometimes we're guilty of knowing all we need to know about someone simply by watching that person step over the curb on her way in. She is still 40 feet away and hasn't spoken a word, yet we gather quick surface assumptions and act on them (or, more often, *don't* act).

Many a sale has been stalled or broken by leading with incorrect assumptions that are based on what someone is wearing, what he's driving, dirt under his fingernails, or his need to pass a comb through his hair. In most cases the downside lies in underestimating the prospect on the basis of appearance.

Most organizations we researched provided similar stories: The real estate agent who did not take a buyer seriously (and treated the buyer that way) finally received an offer significantly above the asking price except that it included the stipulation that the agent personally receive no commission.

Remember in the movie *Pretty Woman* when Julia Roberts goes shopping on Rodeo Drive? She tells the first store clerk, "I have money, really," but it doesn't matter. She isn't dressed appropriately. She doesn't look like she should be shopping there. She is asked to leave. Later in the movie she walks past the same store, loaded down with packages from up the street, stops in, and asks the same clerk, "Are you on commission?" When the clerk replies, "Yes, I am," Julia, barely able to contain herself, gets in the last word: "Big mistake!"

Sometimes a reverse tendency takes over: *over*estimating a customer's value or worth, again with assumptions that are based solely on surface information. We can't tell you how many times in workshops we have salespeople list customers who are important to them only to realize later that they've got an important "customer" on their list who has never spent a cent with them, only calls for a third quote but never buys, only calls for emergency delivery, and is valued only because of size and potential—not their purchases.

This isn't limited to our professional lives. In your personal world, what thinly based assumptions might you make about those of another ethnic

Pauline is a very powerful person. In describing her personality, terms such as "dominant," "extroverted," and "impatient" would all be appropriate. She has been terrifically successful as the president of a 30-person consulting firm, and their work enjoys a reputation for results, efficiency, and value.

After presenting at an industry conference and trade show, Pauline was enjoying the evening's social event. She was approached by a young woman, Triptta, who told her how much she had enjoyed Pauline's presentation earlier in the day. Pauline thanked her but seemed to be scanning the room. Triptta expressed her opinion and asked a question about the presentation's subject matter—not to dispute, simply to clarify. Pauline curtly and arrogantly dismissed what she perceived to be a challenge from someone who lacked authority or credentials in that area.

The next week the business development officer of Pauline's firm received a call from one of the world's largest quick-serve chains. They had been considering offering a single-source, six-figure consulting contract until Pauline's meeting with Triptta, the chain's chief learning officer. The business development officer was informed that the offer was no longer under consideration.

group or religion or even at a social event? What curb qualifying might take place when you first meet an IRS agent, a police officer, or a priest?

The solution is simple: Even when we can't resist forming impressions that are based on very little data, we can still do nothing. We can keep those impressions and opinions where they belong—to ourselves.

Habit 7—Using Tension as a Tool

Also known as "sale ends Saturday."

We all roll our eyes at the television commercials that regularly scream, *"Everything* must go . . . going out of business . . . *no* reasonable offer refused . . . sales ends Saturday." We know from experience that these people have a going out of business sale every week. We know that every week brings us the opportunity to experience "pricing never before offered"—and it leaves us flat. We all have a built-in BS detector.

What is being used here is tension as a sales tool, specifically, the concept of *coercive power.* At its most basic level coercive power is simply brute force— being the biggest, meanest SOB in the valley—and it *can* generate compliance. In sales, coercive power is embodied through the use of tension, and by this we mean intentionally generated discomfort that is intended to push the customer toward a buying decision.

When it is focused on scarcity, the use of tension may produce some short-term revenue, but in the longer term, when customers feel pressured to do something they're not ready to do, they are going to resent it. Telling a customer, "I only have one left," "I'm not sure if I can hold it for you," or "I can't guarantee it will be available next week" can alienate rather than integrate, repel rather than attract.

We understand that we all have operational constraints under which we work and that they may affect the customer's decision. This is understood and allowed for. Yet when the constraints are manufactured, so is the urgency— and so too will be the customer's interpersonal commitment and loyalty to you. This works both ways in the sales relationship as customers often introduce tension as a negotiating tool as well. How do you like it when they do? What does it do to your opinion of how much they understand or care about you in the relationship?

There is a final dynamic relevant to tension within the sales process that also merits some discussion here: speaking when angry. As the fulcrum between the often-competing forces of customer expectations and organiza-

A pulp mill executes several operations in going from tree to paper. Although pulp can be manufactured mechanically or chemically or with a combination of the two, it always begins with an automated process for taking the bark off the tree. This is done by a debarker that uses a powerful abrasive sequence to strip the bark from the pulpwood.

Rex regularly sold tens of thousands of dollars of chain product that was used in the debarking step at the mill owned by one of his clients. They had contacted Rex with an unscheduled order, and he was relieved to get the call. It was the end of the month and the end of the fiscal quarter; he needed the revenue, and he needed it now.

In speccing out the order with his client, Rex saw an opportunity to ensure that the order would be placed in time for that quarter's accrual. Although not asking for the order overnight, the client was clear that they would need it fairly soon and would experience a shutdown of production if they couldn't get it in time. Rex responded, "You're in luck. We've got it, but it doesn't stay in stock that long. As a matter of fact, if we don't have the order within two days, I can't guarantee that it will be available when you do need it." (That wasn't completely true.)

The client said they would call him back the next day, but they never did. They took Rex at his word and knew that their own internal purchasing couldn't work fast enough to have the purchase order on record in 48 hours. They also knew they couldn't risk not being able to get the chain once the PO was in place. They contacted Rex's competitor and arranged to purchase it from that company when they were ready. They have continued to purchase from the competitor because of its responsiveness when they needed it.

■   ■   ■

Mounir, a mechanical engineer by trade and an engineering team leader, had just finished presenting a proposal for his company's involvement with a global automotive manufacturer. They outlined milestones and timing with a detailed Gantt chart, including specific labor estimates required to complete the project as specified by the client.

Steve, the head buyer on the client side, paused for literally 30 seconds for effect. Looking Mounir in the eye, Steve said, "I'm going to give you 30 minutes alone with your team to figure out how to cut your labor estimates by 10 percent. We have still got to have it by the deadline, but we need a reduction if we're going to be able to afford it."

Mounir responded without missing a beat: "Steve, thank you for the opportunity, but we can save you 30 minutes right now. With eight of us, that's four labor-hours we can avoid right off the bat. My team and I discussed this very possibility before coming and agreed that we are at our walk-away point right now. We appreciate the opportunity to bid on this and wish you luck with the project. I choose not to ask my team to work on something that they feel is underspecced to begin with; it wouldn't be fair to them or to you."

Mounir and his team said their good-byes and left. Within hours of returning to the office he received a call from Steve to let him know that they had been selected for the project. "What about the labor estimates?" Mounir asked. Steve said that he had thought the estimate fair and accurate but wanted to "see how far they would go." He was fine with the quotation and wanted to launch the project ASAP.

Mounir was happy about landing the project but had mixed feelings about working with Steve. Could he be trusted?

tional needs, sales and service professionals are often the recipients of pressure from one side and venom from the other.

Salespeople have to depend on others to provide high-quality products, accurate information, and support to do their jobs in representing the company to the customer. Sometimes others drop the ball at the worst possible time. The product doesn't get shipped, the wrong product is shipped, the invoice is wrong, or the product doesn't perform as expected.

The sales representative gets the full force of the customer's anger: "I'm not paying for this. I'll never do business with your company again, and I'll tell everyone I know not to do business with you." In this scenario the salesperson also may take a loss of commission. When yelled at, threatened, and even insulted about something completely out of their control, along with taking a financial hit, even the calmest salespeople can lose their cool.

And what about customers' contributions to tension levels? They may make promises and break them to suit their needs. Remember Tom Cruise in *Jerry Maguire*? As a newly independent sports agent, he was recruiting a young football player. In the parents' home he got a verbal commitment. Tom suggested getting it all in writing, and the father's reply was, "My word is my bond; we don't need a contract." Of course, later they changed their minds and signed with another agent. That might make anyone angry.

Sales is inherently an emotionally charged arena, and anger (too much tension) makes it especially volatile. Look up "volatility" and you'll find concepts such as instability and risk. In chemistry volatility is defined as a measure of how readily a substance vaporizes. How volatile do you want your relationships to be? Anger is rarely only one person's fault in any relationship, but all you have to do to neutralize the volatility is . . . nothing. The solution again lies in *not* doing, in simply omitting (or at least delaying) an angry response.

Habit 8—One-Upping

The constant need to top our conversational partner in an effort to show the world just how smart we are.

We're not sure if this is a deep-rooted psychological insecurity common to our culture or an outgrowth of the ultracompetitive nature of sales in general, but regardless of the source, the urge is there and it pulls us apart. You tell your associate about a painful dental procedure, and she comes right back with an even more detailed recounting of a more serious, more excruciating experience in the chair. Your brother laments his retirement account implosion, and you let him know how much your house has depreciated in the last 12 months. Even in stories with a happy ending—someone recounts a bluebird sale that just flew in the window—we top it with a larger, more lucrative deal.

Probably most damaging, this happens even with those closest and presumably most important to us, for example, when a spouse or loved one comments on what a rough day she has had. What is our response? Do we offer empathetic statements to communicate that we've heard, to indicate that we understand and care deeply for her misery? Nope, we let loose with a tirade to let her know we're even more miserable than she is. We're so filled with the need to win these meaningless contests that we can't let the people in our lives be less fortunate than we are.

Behaviorally, this ineffective habit often comes through in different forms of evaluative listening in which we nod impatiently until the customer is finally done talking, and then begin our response, rebuttal, or revision before the echo of his voice has faded. The irony is that in trying to impress customers or prospects with the extraordinary nature of our lives, the only impression we end up leaving over time is that of a bore—a self-important fool to be avoided.

Sam, a small business owner from New Jersey and a member of Augusta National Golf Club in Georgia, was taking an important client to Augusta for a special round of "client golf." Eager to impress the client, Sam hoped a round at this most prestigious of clubs would cement the relationship. It took him a long time to gain his membership invitation, and he was justifiably proud of it and what it said about him.

As luck would have it, Sam and his client were paired up in a foursome with a corporate chairman well known to anyone who has ever turned on a television. After introductions, the corporate chair suggested a one-dollar Nassau bet to make it fun. Sam responded that at his club in New Jersey they played a twenty-dollar Nassau. Turning to his cart, the chairman kept it friendly by saying, "I don't know if I can afford that; a dollar is fine." He smiled and motioned for Sam and his partner to take the tee.

Sam and his client lost that one-dollar Nassau bet, but there were no hard feelings. In the clubhouse after the round, over cocktails, Sam and the client sat down with their foursome partners to play cards. The chairman suggested playing gin at one tenth of a cent per point. Sam again interrupted by saying, "At our club we play for ten cents a point."

The chairman was silent for a long while. When he did speak, he addressed Sam directly: "Sam, what do you think you're worth?"

Taking it as a challenge, Sam leaned forward a bit and smiled. "Oh, about $30 million."

The chairman paused again, smiled, and said, "How about we cut the cards for that?"

Sam's client wasn't impressed—not favorably, anyway.

Habit 9—Overfamiliarity

The use of inappropriately intimate gestures.

If we habitually insist on a first-name basis or a casual "how are you today, Sam?" with someone we've just cold-called, our behavior will come off as out of sync or unnatural. What may be acceptable in one part of a country, such as calling someone "honey" in certain southern states, may be received as offensive in other areas. The use of first names, though intended to establish or demonstrate rapport, can often cause a disconnect when done too soon. Even generational differences can affect the way we come across in our use of formal versus informal terms.

Note that we aren't referring to another detrimental interpersonal habit: sexual harassment. When we say inappropriately intimate, we mean manners of address, dialogue, or reference that are not commensurate with the relationship at hand.

Familiarity is a matter of interpretation and can be cultural as well. In many languages (the Romance languages come to mind) verbs are conjugated or articles used for formal or informal address of another individual. "*Te agradezco*" and "*le agradezco*" both mean "I thank you" in Spanish, depending on the relationship you perceive you have with the other person. One is informal, the other formal. Physical space and proximity is another cultural variable that when ignored can hinder rather than help the process of staying connected through empathy.

Our message here is simple: Err in the direction of formality. Wait to be invited to use a first name. Too often we feel that sales is about the rush to a relationship, when in fact there has to be a *reason* for two people to build rapport and trust. Just because we *want* there to be trust, rapport, respect, and even affection tying us to our customers, doesn't make it so. Let the relationship build at its own pace, let empathy do its job, and behave in proportion to your customers' definition of your relationship.

It is evening in December at a very popular, very crowded shopping mall. As shoppers pass in couples, singles, and groups, we hear the attention getters that one young kiosk seller is using to establish a connection with uninterested prospects: "Excuse me, miss, do you celebrate Christmas?" The customer picks up her pace to get away. The seller tries with another passerby: "Excuse me, sir, do you love your family?" Incredulous, the gentleman looks her way and shakes his head as he puts more space between them. One last time the seller tries with a twenty-something young man: "Excuse me, sir, are you married?" As happened every other time, she gains eye contact for a moment, but the prospect picks up speed in moving away from, not toward, her. She has yet to get anyone to stop to talk with her about her products.

Habit 10—Withholding Passion and Energy

The tendency to forget that people decide on the basis of emotion and later justify that decision with logic.

As a professional, you believe in what you represent, right? Your product or service offering is very much a part of your personal identity. As a matter of fact, we're wagering you live it and you love it. With this kind of visceral commitment to the value that you bring to the lives of your customers, why is it that some customers find your self-presentation flat, mechanical, disinterested, or even indifferent?

Passion is defined as "a powerful emotion or appetite; boundless enthusiasm; an abandoned display of emotion; fervor; zeal; ardor." There are countless reasons why we tend to withhold passion in our interactions with customers or prospects. It might be that our prospects come to us, for example, at retail in such a way that sometimes we're overwhelmed. It might be that we've sold the same items or services to the same kinds of people for a long, long time. It might even be that certain individuals not only drain your passion but suck the very life out of you.

That's why it's called work—physical or mental effort or activity directed toward production or accomplishment (see labor, toil). We know that there are a million things that can draw down our reserves, but as we've said, it's a lot easier to fix what is wrong than it is to figure out how things got screwed up in the first place.

In fact, let's put a stake in the ground: It doesn't matter *why* we withhold passion in our interactions with others. What matters is understanding that people decide about 80 percent of the time on the basis of emotions; logic is the tipping point in only about 20 percent of purchase decisions. Emotion trumps reason. Let's take it one step further. One Harvard scholar believes that not only are purchase decisions emotionally based, they are due to subconscious motivation 95 percent of the time. Is it possible that only 5 percent of purchase decisions are a prospect's behavior based on rational thought?

How scary is that?

The place is packed tonight. Maria's Italian restaurant is ideally located 500 yards off the freeway between two upscale shopping malls. It's part of a community that is doing very well economically, and at seven o'clock on a Saturday evening, business is good.

People can barely get in the door, and once they do, it takes five minutes just to get to the hostess stand to then find out it is a 50- to 60-minute wait for a table (longer for a booth). Customers are always welcome to enjoy a cocktail in the lounge while they wait, yet with thirsty patrons three-deep at the bar, it is difficult to get a drink.

At the hostess stand Larry and Sharon are working at informing newcomers, timing tables, and handing out "vibrating coasters" to let customers know when their tables are ready. Both are experienced but both appear bored, apathetic, and distant. Several customers near the hostess stand have yet to get eye contact from Larry and Sharon as they discuss the frustrating logistics of their busiest night of the week. The food is really good at Maria's and the location is convenient, yet there appear to be many customers beginning to second-guess their choice.

As we'll discuss in Chapter 8, savvy organizations are measuring what we call a "customer effort score." This essentially measures how much effort a customer has to expend to do business with us. There are very strong correlations between how much effort customers have to put in and subsequent purchase loyalty: The less energy they have to expend, the higher their loyalty to us. Perhaps we need another measure of how much energy *we* expend on their behalf and how that correlates to their loyalty.

We know that unbridled displays of passion don't always work in a sales setting—nor are they always appropriate—but we also know that passion is a catalyst for rapport and empathy. Can you afford to withhold passion and energy at work? Can you afford to withhold it at home?

You decide.

Habit 11—Explaining Failure

Behaving under the erroneous belief that simply being able to assign blame, fault, or guilt is enough to satisfy the customer.

Just as there is no crying in baseball, there are no excuses in sales. Over the last decades we have interviewed thousands of people. How many times do you think we've heard, "I was pretty upset over the fact that you screwed up my order until the salesperson gave me those awesome excuses. As soon as I got the explanation for the failure, I felt so much better."

We don't think we have ever heard it. *Ever.*

Common across both sides of the customer influence aisle (sales *and* service), this annoying tendency usually starts with a mechanical or, worse, condescending explanation of why the customer was let down. As if an intellectual understanding of the organization's functional failure should be enough to get customers to realign their expectations, we dig as deeply as necessary into the operational variables to negate the validity of a customer's complaint.

Simply put, we operate under the incorrect assumption that understanding trumps injury and that if we can all comprehend what went wrong—if we can generate enough plausible detail—the customer no longer has a valid beef. Insult is added to injury when we react with indignation to a customer's continued dissatisfaction (understanding does not trump injury). As with the previously described interpersonal eccentricities, the empathic disconnect caused by explaining failure can be avoided by refraining from the overwhelming desire to explain away a customer's complaint, confusion, or apprehension.

You'll be far more effective focusing not on what went wrong but on what will come—on what you will do next for them.

Emilio has used the same overnight shipping service almost exclusively for over 20 years. There have been a few times when he went with competitive options instead, but for the most part it has been the same envelopes, same two-day boxes, and same paperwork for everything that has had to be there without fail. When he had to use another service because of location or a client requesting it specifically, Emilio always seemed to have problems: It didn't arrive when promised, there were mix-ups about who signed for the package, contents were broken or the packaging crushed—his experiences with the competitors weren't very positive.

That was why his most recent experience with his regular company was so surprising—and disturbing.

Emilio had shipped a second-day package cross-country on a Thursday to arrive on Monday. The package hadn't arrived by first thing Wednesday morning and, thinking it unusual, Emilio called in. The sales and service representative answered quickly and professionally as usual. After explaining the situation and providing the details, Emilio was placed on hold for a moment while the rep did her research. Coming back on the line, the representative asked if she could transfer Emilio to a trace agent, as that person would be tasked with tracking the package.

Emilio was transferred and was told by Alberto, the trace agent, that the package was showing a last scan from the previous Friday and nothing since. He further informed Emilio of the fact that very rarely packages are torn open in automated handling and that they have a special room in each hub city where those damaged packages are kept for investigation. He explained that they have over 18 acres under one roof that is 80 percent mechanized handling and that that was probably the reason the package was missing. Alberto also asked Emilio if he would describe the contents of the two-day box so that they could check inside. Emilio described the contents and was told that Alberto would call him back after investigating.

Emilio knew what probably had happened to the package, but that didn't seem to help. At no point did anyone acknowledge the consequences of the company's functional failure. Emilio didn't mind the package's loss too much. After 20 years of nearly flawless performance, that was understandable and acceptable. It was the fact that the trace agent simply detailed their process and what probably had happened and then closed the call. Emilio came away thinking, "I guess the shippers are all the same after all."

Twenty years of loyalty now at risk.

Habit 12—Never Having to Say You're Sorry

The personal inability to apologize or accept responsibility for personal or organizational error or injury.

A close cousin to explaining failure, the habit of refusing to acknowledge that the customer has been wronged—and refusing to express regret for the customer's loss—is one of the top reasons tension escalates in company-customer interactions.

How do you feel when as a customer your sales contact never quite gets around to saying, "I'm sorry, we goofed"? He provides all the reasons in the world why you didn't get what you paid for, he can recite chapter and verse the company's policy and "recovery" procedures, but still there is never any personal verbal acknowledgment that your disappointment is righteous. How does that leave you feeling?

It could be that we feel that by apologizing we give up power in a relationship (that couldn't be further from the truth). It could also be that our organization is so fearful of litigation or loss of profit in turbulent times that we perceive significant pressure from our bosses to deflect the responsibility that a heartfelt apology implies. In any case, it's as true in professional relationships as it is in personal rapport: The act of expressing remorse and regret is cleansing and empowering for you and for the human connection between you and your customer.

The awesome thing about "I am sorry"—not "I apologize" but "I. Am. Sorry."—is that it opens the door for both parties to let go of the past and move on. The only thing we can control is what we do *now* and what we do *next*. Saying we are sorry allows for the possibility of doing just that.

Aiste has had her own business for 22 years. She is an engineer by education and did her postgraduate work at MIT. Aiste specializes in risk assessment, helping manufacturers minimize their exposure to the human liabilities of their manufacturing processes. She has crafted a niche for herself in consulting and appearing as an expert witness. Approaching middle age, Aiste is very healthy through good nutrition and lots of exercise.

Being self-employed, Aiste has paid her own medical insurance for those 22 years. When she first went out on her own, she picked up a COBRA policy for the first 18 months and then an independent policy for her and her family. Her kids are growing up, and only one is still at home and covered by her policy. She has received a letter from her health insurer stating that because of "reaching a 'milestone birthday,' she might notice a slight increase in her premiums." She sure did—a 48 percent increase!

Are they kidding?

After 30 minutes on the phone with the insurance company's call center, Aiste can't believe the responses she is receiving. "I have been a solid customer for 22 years, and can you personally tell me that you believe that a 48 percent bump is a 'slight increase'?"

The CSSR she is speaking with robotically responds that that is indeed an increase.

"No, I asked, 'Do you believe that to be a *slight* increase?'"

The CSSR does not respond; there is only silence.

Aiste tries another tack: "Are you telling me I have no choice but to pay an additional 48 percent every month?"

"No" replies the CSSR. "You have a choice: You can change your policy."

Aiste is really losing it now. "Yeah, you told me I can lower my coverage or drastically raise my deductible amount yet still experience a 'slight increase' no matter what. I call that no choice at all! Don't you even care one little bit?"

Again, only silence.

Aiste chokes back her initial thought and says, "I can't talk to you any further right now. I've got to call again when I'm not so angry."

To this the CSSR replies: "Okay, thank you for calling. Is there anything else I can help you with at this time?"

This time there is only silence from Aiste.

Habit 13—Throwing Others under the Bus

Sacrificing a colleague—often anonymous, often vulnerable, and usually innocent—by blaming her or him for one's own functional failure.

Although this habit may be driven partly by people's need to explain failure, we believe that this particular version is more personal. Think back for a minute about the joke about two hikers discussing what would happen if they came across a bear on the trail. The joke ends with one hiker saying, "I don't have to run faster than the bear; I just have to run faster than *you.*"

The bear in question here is usually an unhappy customer we've wronged; we failed to deliver what we promised. The customer is upset and is righteously expressing her dissatisfaction. We react immediately (sometimes viscerally) to the tension and look for the easiest, quickest escape route (or, more on target, escape-*goat*). What better release than deflecting the tension onto someone else, someone unnamed and not present who is often irrelevant to the interaction at hand. We find someone else to sacrifice to the bear.

We don't like it when it happens to us (how many times have you heard a salesperson say, "They shouldn't have told you that?"). How trustworthy can someone so lacking in loyalty to his or her organization or colleagues be to represent you as the customer in the equation? When it comes time for that person to stand up and represent you so that you receive promised value, how comfortable are you that you won't end up with heavy-duty tire tracks up and down your back?

This habit deserves special attention in that it truly is a hybrid of several habits—with a fairly easy out. It is made up of equal parts tendency to explain failure, simple refusal to apologize, and the uncontrollable urge to say something (vocal filler), and the fix is relatively simple and a hybrid as well: Bite back your urge to speak without forethought. Say nothing except "I'm sorry."

How tough is that? It costs you nothing. It communicates that you have heard and understood the customer. It communicates a willingness to accept responsibility for failure *and* for resolution. It builds and maintains the interpersonal connection between you and your customer. It is money in the bank.

Gustav is a regional sales director for a large distribution firm. He has several account managers who work for him and does his best to coach and develop those who desire the guidance. Today's focus is not on development. With one of his account managers, Amy, he has noticed not only a drop in reaching sales targets but also a significant rise in customer complaints. He's decided on a "ride with" to accompany Amy to her customer meetings today.

As they've driven to and between appointments, he's listened in on Amy's side of several phone conversations and hasn't liked what he's heard: "You mean Sarah didn't send that over? Darn, she promised me she would." "Raul didn't follow up with you? He told me personally that he did; I can't believe he lied."

When Gustav and Amy meet with the purchasing department of a sizable customer, the client asks about the quotation that was promised for the previous week. Gustav remains silent and closely watches Amy, who says, "I'm sorry that didn't go out. We've been having problems at the service center getting quotes out; yours is not the first. Again, I'm sorry. I'll get on them as soon as we get back today."

Gustav has seen enough.

He doesn't mention a thing on the short drive back to the office. He first checks with accounting on the quotation that was delinquent. Amy had never turned in the quotation for processing. After calling the client, he pulls in human resources and legal and explores what Amy's behavior has been doing not just to her results but to the morale of the team and, even more important, the relationship with the client.

Amy is fired within the week.

Habit 14—Propagandizing

Overreliance on organizational rhetoric and themes.

Propaganda can be loosely defined as a plan for spreading ideas and beliefs to large numbers of people. Every organization has its propaganda, and with good reason. You can't possibly reach thousands (or millions) of customers with a consistent product or service without a consistent message. This is Marketing 101, and to do this, at some point someone has to write down the desired message and communicate it throughout the organization. This plan for disseminating information in a systemic fashion allows for consistency, critical mass, and momentum in the delivery of a product or service.

So where do difficulties arise? Where do ineffective interpersonal habits creep into the equation? We think that occurs when we ask our people, our sales and service providers, not to think and not to adapt to dynamic customer needs or customers' level of readiness to buy, but simply to regurgitate the company line. We talked before about organizational efforts to remove the human being from the customer-company interface. We see it everywhere, and where we don't see it, we see human beings forced to respond with rote, repetitive, out-of-context, meaningless, scripted *booyah!*

Imagine that it's dinnertime at home. You've just begun to relax from a long day when the phone rings, and you pick it up only to have the person on the other end begin a scripted conversation ("How are you tonight, Mr. Wilson?"). Sometimes, depending on your day, you might listen for anywhere from 10 to 30 seconds until the well-meaning rep finally has to take a breath, and then what do you do? In our workshops we hear everything from "I hand the phone to my four-year-old," or "I switch to Spanish," to some take on Seinfeld's response of "How about you give me your home number and I'll call you back later this evening."

Universally we resent the call: first the personal intrusion and then the personal insult of the repeating (if not literally the reading) of lines scripted for the purpose of duping us into spending money or divulging information that we will wish we hadn't.

Russell is purchasing a new vehicle. He's purchased several before, so this isn't a brand-new experience for him. He is a brand-loyal individual and has bought from this dealership before. The sales consultant is new to Russell as his previous consultant has left the dealership.

After they select the specific vehicle together, the sales consultant asks if he can introduce Russell to their F&I manager to cover "finance and insurance." Although Russell is paying cash for the truck, he agrees to speak with her while the sales consultant runs the paperwork through his manager.

The F&I manager's name is Olga. She greets Russell warmly and thanks him for purchasing from them again. She suggests he take a seat and begins by asking him how he's enjoyed his last vehicles with the brand. Listening intently, she continues asking if he is aware of longer-term repair data on the truck he's planning to purchase. Before Russell can respond, she opens a portfolio on the desk that depicts repair and preventive maintenance estimates at each mileage level over the course of ownership.

Put off, Russell asks, "Are you trying to sell me an extended warranty?"

Olga defensively responds, "Oh, no. I just wanted to make sure you were familiar with the latest information on what downstream ownership costs are for your truck."

"Right," Russell says. "I just happened to come and 'meet' the F&I manager. You just 'coincidentally' had a four-color brochure of ownership expenses versus warranty packages. No thank you. You can tell whoever you need to that you put me through the presentation; just say I wasn't interested."

Russell decides to wait for the final paperwork in the customer lounge, wondering whether he has made the right choice.

Some individuals have the ability to cover all the desired points without reading a script, without having it sound like a premeditated conversation. Even the most gifted of us, if we aren't careful, eventually fall into the trap of relying on the company line as a secondhand stand-in for genuine conversation.

Why does it happen? Think about the conditions under which we exist. Our organizations inundate us with communication. Most of us are under constant pressure to propagate any one of several messages. In short, we get *numb.* We hear the words over and over and spit them back out in the false confidence that the fulfillment of organizational directives will result in the fulfillment of customer needs.

Perhaps this is another hybrid habit, hand in hand with selective hearing; propagandizing, like any other behavior, can be value-neutral in and of itself. It occurs when we overuse the message, when we engage in what one colleague called "premature elaboration," when we mismatch the message to the prospect, or when we substitute the use of prepared nuggets of wisdom for genuine conversation.

That is when the customer perceives it as another annoying habit that gives the profession of sales a bad name. Proper preparation means that you have rehearsed an interaction mentally, but the most professional and effective among us (like the best actors who can deliver their lines over and over) converse naturally, instinctively, and enthusiastically.

Habit 15—Wasting Energy

Taking part in organizational blame-storming and pity parties.

These last two habits are very special. They are not transactional—they do not take place in front of your customer. Their effects, however, bleed over into your interactions and relationships with your customers. They are often a root cause rather than a symptom of the ineffective habits that destroy empathy and rapport.

Our first bonus habit, wasting energy, is manifested by engaging in activities that are not only *un*productive but also *counter*productive. We mentioned corporate blame-storming and pity parties. The question is how *much* time—and energy—do you spend joining in at lunch or at the water cooler, in the break room, or cafeteria when the topic is who screwed up or who did what to whom for what reason?

What do you get out of these "discussions"? You spend time and invest significant amounts of energy for what return? Do you gain a competitive edge in the marketplace? Are you gaining rapport or maintaining connections with your customers? Chances are that you gain nothing and waste the most precious resource you have: your emotional energy and mental shelf space.

During an important interview, one chief executive in a contracting industry was asked why her organization was flourishing while competitors were crashing. Her response: "I'm not reading newspapers, and I seriously limit my access to cable or online news. I need the energy elsewhere." This seemingly offhand remark says a great deal about what it will take to "get you there."

We have unlimited options in terms of gathering "news": liberal options, conservative options, options in between. We can literally spend all day—24 hours each day—passively watching the world go by around us on TV. We can do it at work too. There are unlimited opportunities to engage in counterproductive, judgmental, usually destructive and often vicious, vindictive conversations around just about any topic.

Sherman and Lynne had worked for the same company for at least five years. Both had earned their graduate degrees and were well compensated, and most would agree that their work was challenging, engaging, and meaningful. Their organization had gone through several rounds of job elimination over the last two years. Each time cuts were announced, the message from management was, "This is the team that will carry us into the future." Through each round of reductions more jobs were eliminated, and the demands and expectations placed on those that were left continued to go up.

Now the son of the company's owner was being brought in to "save the legacy." His style of accusation, condemnation, and proclamation was pushing morale deeper into darkness. Although Lynne didn't smoke, Sherman did, and the two could often be found outside the loading dock discussing the latest news. While Sherman would feed his tobacco habit, Lynne would tell him about what she had heard from accounting or customer support. Both would voice not only their opinion of the damage the last change had wrought but also a guess as to what the next damage would be.

If you were to assess the loss every day, you would find the two spent perhaps 30 to 40 minutes outside every morning and another 30 to 40 in the afternoon. Two people, 60 to 80 minutes every day, five days a week—it adds up to 50 to 60 hours of lost productivity every month to the organization. We also wonder how much it added up to in lost commissions and bonuses for Sherman and Lynne, and they weren't the only employees out there.

Sales *is* a high-energy profession. Interacting with other human beings takes focus, time, energy, and attention. If you use it elsewhere, you won't have it for your customers.

You won't have it for those who matter in your life, either.

Habit 16—Obsessing over the Numbers

Achieving revenue, profit, or productivity targets at the expense of metrics of a higher calling.

Is it possible to be too focused on objectives, on numbers? Can goal obsession be a bad thing even in sales? Goal obsession presents a dilemma that many people fail to consider. On the one hand, the single-minded focus on making one's numbers is admired, encouraged, and often specifically incentivized. It's tough to knock someone who refuses to accept less than perfect results. On the other hand, at what cost do we hit the target? What price is acceptable in exchange for leading the sales board?

An obsession with making the numbers can lead to two significant errors in judgment: in what *we* want from life and in what we believe *others* want from us.

In the first case we follow the logic-emotion train of thought that if we can just achieve our goals, we'll make more money, provide better for our loved ones, have more free time, enjoy life more, and in general be happier. Admirable, right? Yet in the pursuit we end up living out of the present, always just a bit out in the future (I just need *one* more good month). We also often ignore or even injure those important to us.

We alienate our customers or at least take the best ones for granted. We miss every one of our kids' soccer, basketball, or volleyball games. But we make the number. We end up with a hollow imitation of what we thought we wanted—success, but at what price?

In the case of misunderstanding what others want from us, we can be led even further astray. Our boss sets a target for us—revenue growth, profitability, you name it—and we want to hit it. Our significant other would like to be able to afford more space for the family. Great motivator of performance, right? Yet in the pursuit we begin to hold back certain information from our clients to make the sale. We start to redefine what a lie is in the interest of moving revenue up or holding it off until later.

In the pursuit, we walk all over our coworkers in ways big and small. We steal a deal here, cheat a lead generation there. We've even known sales profes-

C A S E   S T U D Y

Bruce was an account director for a custom video production house. Producing communications and training for a number of Fortune 500 organizations, Bruce's team was known for award-winning work and sound, profitable project management. Within his own organization Bruce was a founding member of the project management association that met regularly to work with the entire creative team to design and implement processes and procedures that would improve the whole company's output.

One day Bruce was calling on Ernst, a client who had been his contact on several previous projects. All had been very successful: on time, on budget, and extremely well received. They were discussing Ernst's plans for a new communications network blending Web-based, e-mail, and synchronous live events to get the word out to their members on product, competencies, and marketing campaigns.

As they discussed specifications for the message delivery, Ernst casually mentioned that it unfortunately had to be a competitive bid process and that Bruce's competitor had put Ernst's wife in their bid for a $10,000 consulting fee.

Bruce didn't really hear the comment. He was so busy calculating and recording specs and budget that the phrase "put my wife in for a consulting fee" didn't register until the ride home. While driving back after the meeting, Bruce thought, "Wait a minute, they put his 'wife' in for a $10,000 consulting fee . . . for what? As far as I know, Ernst has never mentioned that his wife was in our business. I don't know what they would have her do that would be worth $10,000. I think I've just been asked for a bribe . . . to *buy* the business!"

Bruce's company didn't get the contract for the communications network. He did not include a $10,000 budget item for Ernst's wife. In fact, Bruce's team never again did any work with Ernst's organization.

sionals to come into the office at midnight to see what leads came in on the fax or Internet since closing time. We begin to venture far outside our value set—and we make the numbers. Are we true to what others want of us? Would our children be proud of our being able to provide a larger home? Perhaps. Would they be proud of how we were able to afford it?

Goal obsession. Making the numbers. It cuts both ways. Periodic personal time out such as the time you're taking to read this book can give you extra insurance to make sure that you are taking a shot at reaching the right numbers, in the right way.

So What? What did you learn?

- Shifting into neutral: try doing nothing.
- These habits are not flaws of skill, intelligence, or personality.
- This isn't a religious conversion. All that's required is the guts to stop doing some of what you've done in the past.

Now What? What might you do now?

- Make a note of what habit or habits jump out at you as what might be holding you back (there's no commitment here; it's just a matter of capturing your first impressions while they're fresh).
- Show the list of habit titles in the book to someone whose opinion you trust (at work or at home) and ask that person what you are most guilty of. Then ask that person which habit he or she is most guilty of. Don't take it any further than that right now; just begin to consider the habits and how they affect you.

To the Veteran Seller: The Comfort Paradox

That was quite a list: 16 habits that when considered together give the sales profession a really bad name that give the human race a really bad name. Take a deep breath . . . let it out. Think back to what we said at the end of Chapter 6: This is not about skill, intelligence, personality, or a deep religious conversion. It is about making some simple behavioral changes in your life.

Before putting you on the road to selecting which habit you might want to give up first for your customers, we'll give you some time to reflect. Take some time to soak up a little of what we've learned about these habits not just from our observations but directly from some of the pros we went to for answers.

THE VOICE OF *OUR* CUSTOMER

We've already mentioned that as we researched and developed this content, we spoke to hundreds of "buyers," some within our own customers' organizations and many within organizations that were new to us. As we learned more about the habits that hold people back in sales, two distinct categories regularly emerged in our interviews: *sales veterans* and *sales rookies.*

It is universally recognized that the veteran salesperson is unquestionably a unique case with several identifiable tendencies when it comes to ineffective habits with his or her customers. The salesperson newer to the game also was felt to exhibit predictable tendencies, and in fact a new, very special breed of salesperson has been born: the sales "draftee." There is now a sizable contingent of salespeople who never intended or wanted to become salespeople. These draftees have been brought into the sales force by economic, organizational, and cultural factors beyond their control, and they're here to stay.

In many arenas, service has turned to sales. We had a workshop participant who said, "I am an engineer because I don't really like dealing with people, and now they've made me a customer service engineer." We have had others in customer education in the medical equipment industry, all clinical people from registered nurses to medical doctors, who were told by their organizations, "You used to be in medicine; now you're in sales." From call centers to automotive dealerships, traditional service providers are being asked, and paid, to sell.

In this chapter and the next, you will have our thoughts and observations around the tendencies of each of these populations, along with transcripts of a few of our interviews with the likes of Nike's director of sales, Abbott Vascular's global vice president of sales, the retail sales improvement manager for the Ford Customer Service Division, and an executive vice president of operations who deploys no less than 54,000 sales and service agents around the globe. Before selecting an ineffective habit to attack, take some time to absorb our observations on the habits of these two most common sales populations and then soak up the unfiltered voices of those who manage these dynamic populations for a living.

THE SALES VETERAN

To begin, let's explore what makes someone a sales veteran and then consider some of the relevant trends that affect a veteran's world every day. We'll also look at the interpersonal habits that a veteran of sales may be most likely to commit.

Across several industries there seemed to be no set time frame that would make someone a sales veteran. Lots of studies have been done to determine how long it takes a salesperson to become "productive" but none to determine how long it takes to become a veteran. What we heard without exception is that it takes repeated, consistent high levels of revenue performance. The time it takes, we believe, is relative to the industry or even the company. From what we heard, you can plan on three to seven years of meeting and exceeding *real* targets, even with more than one employer, to earn you the title of sales veteran.

Whether extolling the numbers that come in or the way minds are moved, many of the descriptors used for a sales pro or sales vet revolved around the theme of *consciousness and competence.* The pro or veteran of sales in most cases would be described as someone who has gotten to the point of making sales happen "unconsciously"—without thought or awareness of exactly what she was doing at the time. "All I have to do is give them the bullets and they will hunt!" was the way one manager described the dynamic. We agree, with one provision: We'd like to bring consciousness back to selling. We would like to reintroduce *acting on purpose.*

The idea of *un*conscious competence can of course work for us, but just as often it has the potential to work against us. The same confident, experienced individual who has seen it all in selling, the same vet who has stepped on and around all the mines in the minefield, can make miracles without thinking or just as easily unconsciously retire on the job. Without warning, these individuals become too comfortable, lose their drive and enthusiasm, and unknowingly embody the antithesis of what we were hoping for. This is *the paradox of comfort:* The very dynamics of time and experience that make a salesperson a veteran of sales may or may not make that person the sales pro all of us hope to deal with. The vision of significant experience and competence, along with a *beginner's mindset,* is what captures the essence of what would make a vet . . . a pro.

What are the relevant trends that affect sale pros according to those who manage them every day?

- Information
- The use of information technology

■ Sell-through concepts
■ The evolution of customers

In earlier chapters we discussed the impact of the access our customers have to information today and what a difference it makes that we, as salespeople, are no longer the only expert source. The last three bulleted points above are related and relevant to the sales pro in that across the board, customers are evolving. Buying power has shifted in many cases from individuals to groups and committees. In some instances we now sell directly to our customers and through to *their* customers as well. These sell-through realities force us to leverage technologies to understand and gain access to these second-tier customer groups.

What habits do we find to be the most common ineffective behaviors for the seasoned sales veteran? The consensus seems to be:

■ **Habit 1: Failure to be present**—repeated and annoying displays of behavior that indicate that we would rather be somewhere else, some-*when* else, or with someone else.
■ **Habit 4: Selective hearing**—the absence of active listening in the presence of the customer.
■ **Habit 6: Curb qualifying**—the tendency to judge a prospect's means and motive superficially from a distance.
■ **Habit 7: Using tension as a tool**—also known as "sale ends Saturday."
■ **Habit 8: One-upping**—the constant need to top our conversational partner in an effort to show the world just how smart we are.
■ **Habit 10: Withholding passion and energy**—the tendency to forget that people decide on the basis of emotion and later justify that decision with logic.

Although we feel these habits have no monopoly in usage by veterans of the art of selling, we believe you will find that they come up more often than not in that group. What most of veterans seem to have in common is the "dark side" of having seen it all. When a particular interaction is not your first but your thousand and first, the unconscious tendency can be to check out of the interaction, believing that you understand a person or that person's needs without expending or investing your own energy or passion. A customer can speak only about one-third as fast as we can listen (or pretend to), think, and formulate. We often can maintain interactions with only a small amount of our interpersonal capacity involved.

Another dynamic common to the habits sales veterans fall into is directly related to their long-term exposure to the highly competitive nature of sales. Although competition and pressure to perform can be healthy (and when you aren't paid unless someone buys, you know pressure unimaginable to those not in sales), it also can lead veterans of sales to try to compete with their own customers. The habits of one-upping and using tension as a tool usually result from our need to win not only on our own terms but now.

But don't just take our word for it. What follows are interviews we conducted with two very special pros in the sales game: John McLean, director of U.S. sales for Nike Golf (equipment and footwear), and Chris Richardson, vice president—global sales with Abbott Vascular.

John McLean, Director of Sales — NIKE

Although currently with Nike, John has spent the last 15 years living at the top of the sales ranks of TaylorMade–Adidas Golf and Acushnet–Cobra Golf. Setting records in revenue, margin dollars, and margin percentages for his employers, John knows the world of sales.

What Got You Here (**WGYH**): Okay, first question: Can you give us the *Readers Digest* version of your career in sales and sales management through the years?

McLEAN: I've been extremely fortunate to have spent the last 15 years in the golf industry. In 1996, after six months of pursuit, I left a good-paying job as a project engineer in the construction industry and accepted my first opportunity in sales as a customer service–inside sales rep for TaylorMade Golf. While selling over the phone isn't what I would consider a long-term career aspiration, I knew it would be a necessary entry point into golf, and it certainly gave me great perspective and training. This was the beginning of my new sales career.

After earning my first outside sales territory in Los Angeles, I began to set goals for where I ultimately wanted to be. For the next 14 years, I gained invaluable experience as a sales rep on the East and West coasts and in management as a regional manager, strategic account manager, and head of U.S. sales with two separate companies. Like many industries, the golf business has seen perpetual change over the years and will continue to evolve. Today, as director of U.S. sales for Nike Golf, I place tremendous weight on my previous work experience to make decisions that will ultimately help achieve the best results for our company.

WGYH: Well, thank you, John. What kinds of trends do you see coming in selling and sales?

McLEAN: First of all, product and product knowledge is king. Before you even start talking about sales, you must have great-performing products. Consumers want great-performing products, and the bar continues to be raised. Specific to sales and selling in our industry, training the retail sales staff is really vital. With the Internet and the amount of information that is at the fingertips of any consumer, the importance has never been greater for the sales staff selling *your* products to be informed and thoroughly aware of *your* selling points (remember, they aren't just selling our product, and if they are not comfortable speaking to our features and benefits, we will not be part of the consideration set, which means the customer will never see our product).

WGYH: Is there anything else that differentiates selling for you today?

McLEAN: Yes, the focus on sell-through initiatives. You know, 10 years ago when I was a sales rep, it was all about selling product in the highest quantity you could. But in today's world, business practices are dramatically different. Retailers have evolved and are much better at managing their business; they have to be or they won't be around very long. Inventory turns and margin rates are common conversation topics. In addition, most retailers are understaffed; golf professionals are wearing several hats and have more responsibilities than they ever have. As a result of these shifts, the amount of inventory a retailer is willing and able to carry is less, and greater turn rates become essential for us to grow our business. Consequently, our sales team needs to spend a greater proportion of their time focused on sell-through and service initiatives such as merchandising the store, club fitting, and product demo days. In many cases, we are doing the selling to our customers' customers. Some golf manufacturers are now starting to place their own employees inside of the larger retail stores to help with that.

WGYH: Makes sense, which kind of leads us into another question: Are there any trends in buying that you are seeing or that you see coming?

McLEAN: Just that the consumers are really looking for value. They want a great product for a great price. The Internet is becoming a bigger and bigger piece of the early sales process, which makes the one-on-one interactions when they do come into a retail location that much more important. The customer often still wants to talk to someone face to face at some point during the buying process.

WGYH: What do you love about sales, John?

McLEAN: Sales is black and white. Either you get the sale or you don't; you either achieve your targets or you don't. I like that; everything is just right out there in the open.

WGYH: John, what is it in your mind that makes the sales veteran different?

McLEAN: The sales veteran typically has been doing it a bit longer. They're more polished in their conversations; they typically have (or develop) better relationships, especially if they've been in the same territory for some time. Veterans don't let the small things get in the way; they confidently focus on what matters, and they are certainly more efficient and effective with whatever tools and resources the company is providing.

WGYH: You gave a pretty good list there about communication, relationships, and competence. I guess another question would be, What does it take for a rep to attain that veteran status?

McLEAN: First and foremost, it's maturity in the role, and it takes time.

WGYH: When you look at sales veterans, what do they bring to the organization?

McLEAN: Certainly confidence and their knowledge coupled with efficiency; speed is so critical these days in business. You can almost always count on your veterans to deliver.

WGYH: You bet, which leads us to this: Is there a weakness that you can think of? What kind of weaknesses would a sales veteran have?

McLEAN: Certainly if someone has been doing it a long time, just complacency, just hitting their numbers or staying in the middle of the pack. Another would be just losing the drive.

WGYH: In reference to the 16 habits that our customers want us to give up, are there some that veterans are more guilty of than others?

McLEAN: Withholding passion is probably the biggest veteran mistake. It's not intentional; it just happens to many who have been very successful for a long time. Even when you're winning a lot, the excitement dulls.

WGYH: Would there be any of those habits that veteran reps are least guilty of?

McLEAN: Selling past the close. You learn the danger early on. Just lose one sale that way, and you mature and understand that it's not necessary, that it can hinder a sale versus help it.

WGYH: Are there any interpersonal habits that we might have missed that would be specific to the sales veteran when you think of what gets *your* seasoned veterans in trouble?

McLEAN: I believe the most important of all is having a beginner's mindset. The people who act like they know it all and are unwilling to change are the ones who get in trouble. It ties back to the maturity thing. If you are a seasoned vet yet maintain a beginner's mindset, *that* is when you truly become great!

Christopher Richardson, Vice President Global Sales— Abbott Vascular

Chris Richardson started out in medicine. At one time a cardiovascular physician's assistant, Chris decided for himself that the world of sales was where he wanted to do his life's work. His training and background as a PA gave him valuable credibility and rapport with his early customers: cardiovascular surgeons. Developing his sales career through Baxter, Guidant Corporation, Boston Scientific, and now Abbott, Chris moved from the district, territory, and regional levels to his current global sales responsibilities.

WGYH: With such a strong background and wealth of experience, what can you tell us about the trends you see coming in sales and selling?

RICHARDSON: The trends we are seeing generally start in buying and then roll down to a selling consequence. One of the strongest trends in medical sales today is truly understanding who your buyer is. The surgeon or cardiologist who used to purchase our products has "lost the prescription pad," we like to say. In so many cases, they can't make the decision anymore, and it is now up to committees or groups of people that have taken over the purchasing or buying decision. I think the trends in health care in general are currently economic in nature. With uncertainty comes caution, and with caution comes delay. This is not necessarily compatible with the inherent urgency of sales.

WGYH: You moved from medicine into sales. That's quite a switch, and you said you did it on purpose. What do you love about sales?

RICHARDSON: What I love about sales is the influence process. The beauty of moving minds, believing in what you do and what you sell and seeing someone you care about move from point A to point B—and hopefully to points C and D down the road. There is poetry in watching a sales pro do his or her thing.

WGYH: Is there anything you really don't like about sales?

RICHARDSON: I guess it might be the travel at times. It's such a global market for us, but outside sales in general is on the move. Whether you're traveling a smaller territory or covering the globe, you're not home; you're on the move. It's face-to-face that really matters in any sales—if you aren't there, someone else will be. It's such a high-energy profession, and "movement" is a constant.

WGYH: What makes the sales veteran different?

RICHARDSON: The sales veteran has been around enough to have found the land mines over and over again, sometimes seeing them and sometimes stepping on them. It's that business maturity to have seen enough transactions, to get to the point where they are consciously competent. They are aware of what they are doing.

WGYH: What makes one a veteran?

RICHARDSON: I don't know if there is really a point at which it happens. There's probably no direct sign, just repeated, consistent excellent performance—until you know it.

WGYH: Chris, what might be the greatest strength of the sales vet?

RICHARDSON: Continuity, continually bringing results, period. Veterans can and will do it for you. I know no one is perfect, but *almost* without fail the sales vet comes through.

WGYH: What might be their biggest weakness?

RICHARDSON: They get too comfortable, too sure. They no longer step up for the team or for the enterprise; they become satisfied with lesser effort.

WGYH: In reviewing the ineffective habits in Chapter 6, which habits do the veterans of sales seem to be most guilty of, and why?

RICHARDSON: I think it would have to be curb qualifying, where the rep doesn't take the time and energy to work with each and every client each and every time—they try to take shortcuts. Selective hearing is another for the very same reason—they believe they can do it with one ear tied behind their back. Withholding passion and energy really resonates along with failure to be present as examples of what happens when veteran sellers get too comfortable in their role—and with their success.

WGYH: For most of those in sales today, Chris, what is the number one thing to stop doing in front of the customer?

RICHARDSON: If there were a universal customer, which there isn't, but let's suppose there were for a moment, I guess it would have to do with your habit 5: contact without purpose. *Stop* coming in without a purpose. Understand that as a salesperson you are there to influence them to buy or use what you bring to the table, yet you are *so* mistaken if you think that they are there to just fill a spot in your schedule for the afternoon. If you have no purpose for the contact from their perspective, you have no business selling to them.

WGYH: For that same group, then, what should they then start doing in front of the customer?

RICHARDSON: This doesn't always happen in front of the customer, but to combat the purposeless contact, *preparing for contact* is paramount. Understanding who the customers are, what their needs are, what the time together would be best suited for; there is often so little of it anymore (time together) that we need to make better use of it than ever. It starts with the generation and expression of purpose.

WGYH: What should they continue doing when in contact with the customer?

RICHARDSON: Bringing value! It is such a pleasure to watch the pro, the professional veteran coming down the hall—and the customer visibly picks up pace walking *toward* them: What have you got for me today? What are you going to tell me? What are you going to show me? Every time I see you, I profit from it. That's magic to see in any sales environment!

WGYH: What is the biggest change we will see over the coming years? Is the game going to be any different?

RICHARDSON: Absolutely. Things will be worlds different—and the difference will be time and information. First, the customer is so much better educated, and the salesperson will be hard-pressed to bring the value equation of information anymore. Second, people just won't have the time to spend with you anymore. For the most part, there will no longer be discretionary time as we know it.

WGYH: In closing, what else should we have asked about?

RICHARDSON: Perhaps just the idea of personal development. You guys do such a great job of raising the bar for us, but we don't seem to take the time, money, or focus to develop ourselves anymore. With the lack of differentiation in most markets today, and products themselves not bringing inherent value to the equation, it's up to the sales pro to add that value. If we're not taking that time to develop ourselves, that's when we fall into ineffective habits—into lost sales ultimately.

So What? What did you learn?

- The special needs of sales veterans versus rookies
- The emergence of the sales draftee
- Relevant trends to the veteran salesperson: information, technology, sell-through, customer evolution
- The paradox of comfort: It can work for you or against you
- Habits that the vet might fall into: failure to be present, selective hearing, curb qualifying, using tension as a tool, one-upping, withholding passion and energy

Now What? What might you do now?

- Take a moment to consider whether your sales arena is populated with veterans or draftees.
- What about you? Does the paradox of comfort affect your productivity?
- Discuss the comfort paradox with your boss. What is her assessment of its impact on you?

When Service Turns to Sales: The Power of Mindset

8

Chapter 7 gave us a lot to consider. The very comfort that comes to a sales veteran after years of experience can trigger either automatic performance or unthinking arrogance. Comfort can engender effective empathetic connections or a repeated disconnect from myriad ineffective interpersonal habits. It is the difference between a sales pro and an annoying veteran.

Now let's take a look at the other end of the experience continuum: the sales novice who maybe never wanted to be in selling in the first place. Countless industries are drafting service providers into sales; it's happening in call centers, car dealerships, medical and dental offices, and even on airplanes (U.S. airlines are bringing in as much as 8 percent of revenue from items other than tickets).

Our collective economy and culture has brought about this conscription into the ranks of sales because more conventional methods of reaching out are either impractical or illegal. The shift from landline phones to cellular, the advent of "do not call," and the expense of traditional mailings have created the need to find some other way to reach out and touch someone. Also, at the same time all this was developing, the ranks of service providers exploded.

In call centers, customers already were making contact; they already were calling us. In car dealerships, customers already were calling in to schedule vehicle maintenance. In professional offices around the world, we already had service providers in regular scheduled contact with our customers. It seems like a natural fit, doesn't it? We need to reach out and sell in a new way, and we have a human resource on the payroll that already gives us the new conduit to the customer: Let's turn service into sales! Thousands of service providers become salespeople overnight. We can't lose, right?

Perhaps. Whereas the single determining variable for the effectiveness of a sales veteran seems to be comfort, we found *mindset* to be the success fulcrum for salespeople new to the game. Would you like to make a guess about the mindset toward sales of those drafted into sales? During workshops we regularly ask sales draftees to play a word association game around the term "salesperson." Easily 95 percent of the terms they associate with that term are not just negative but derogatory. Many have been pulled into a profession that they find, for them, dishonest and distasteful.

Remember that mindset is more than a simple opinion or point of view. It is the foundational set of assumptions we have about the world around us, and those assumptions are the genesis of our behaviors. There is good news, though. Some organizations have found a way to tap in to the base assumptions of their service providers to move them from service to sales. They have done this by transferring the service provider's focus from problems or issues to people and by separating the customer's service agenda from the sales agenda. Where we find disaffected salespeople, we find organizations simply dumping sales pressures on top of the duties of service and satisfaction (at times even competing with service and satisfaction objectives). Where we find an effective transition from service to sales, we see a partnership using solid, compatible analytics and, more important, an honest acknowledgment of the task at hand.

What are the relevant trends that have seemed to drive and affect this movement from service to sales?

■ Technology and the evolution of communication
■ Economics

The development of the customer contact technologies of voice recognition, real-time on-screen delivery of customer data, market penetration, and sales conversion analytics—even social media—has contributed to the utilization of those technologies in up-selling, cross-selling and "service-to-selling." Economics has contributed to this surge of unconventional outbound selling in that the methods work; organizations are achieving results by using them. Whether it is automotive manufacturers using Facebook for new product introduction, airlines gaining an extra $8 billion by up-selling preferred seats and other amenities, or retailers pressing for "extended warranties" and "fabric protection," organizations are desperate to maintain quarterly dividends and are concerned with the short-term financial horizon. Right or wrong, this is what drives the service-to-sales dilemma.

With these organizational dynamics, what habits do we find to be the most common ineffective behaviors for the sales rookie and particularly the new draftee?

■ **Habit 2: Vocal filler**—the overuse of unnecessary (and meaningless) verbal qualifiers.
■ **Habit 3: Selling past the close**—the irresistible urge to verbalize and execute every possible step in the sales process.
■ **Habit 11: Explaining failure**—behaving under the erroneous belief that simply being able to assign blame, fault, or guilt is enough to satisfy the customer.
■ **Habit 12: Never having to say you're sorry**—the personal inability to apologize or accept responsibility for personal or organizational error.
■ **Habit 13: Throwing others under the bus**—sacrificing a colleague—often anonymous, often vulnerable, and usually innocent—by blaming him or her for the one's own functional failure.
■ **Habit 14: Propagandizing**—overreliance on organizational rhetoric and themes.

As with any ineffective habit, rookies and draftees are not the only ones who engage in these behaviors, but the bad habits are grouped together for a reason. We believe that two key factors drive the ineffective habits common to those new to sales or those forced into sales: greater levels of *discomfort or unease with interpersonal tension* and, perhaps because of this, susceptibility to a more *literal adherence to organizational directives and processes.*

When we are new to a task, most of us experience a healthy level of apprehension simply because it *is* new to us. Add to that the nature of sales—pressure to meet targets, consequences associated with real-time success or failure, the unpredictability of human beings (specifically the ones we need to influence)—and it is no wonder that our mindset might work against us. Let's throw one more dynamic on top of all of this: the additional pressure and tension involved when someone is coerced into the role.

What can result is resistance, discomfort, and perhaps less than fertile ground for developing new skills or competencies. In Chapter 4 we discussed the balance of empathy and ego critical to effective influence. Usually in sales the interpersonal deficit is on the empathy side: too much ego and not enough empathy to balance it. Sometimes those new to sales, especially those drafted into it, experience problems resulting from having not enough ego drive and strength. Think about it. With the resilience of ego required, it should be no surprise when we resort to less than effective behaviors to lower our tension.

The second factor affecting this group could be grasping and holding on to organizational safety nets to deflect the interpersonal tension. When we see salespeople engaging in explaining failure, throwing others under the bus, and especially propagandizing, it is often nothing more than using process as a coping mechanism for the rising tension with which they are uncomfortable. Habit 12—the inability to say "I am sorry"—has roots more often than not in the tension between seller and customer *and* between seller and company. We have had participants tell us that they feel no responsibility to apologize when "it's the *company's* fault" that the error occurred in the first place. Sometimes they are able to say "I apologize," but saying "I am sorry" is just too personal for them.

We have observed these dynamics directly by training thousands of sales professionals and their managers in our workshops over the years. We also have had the unique opportunity to interview senior executives for this book. They have managed their organizations to avoid these traps and have been gracious enough to share what they've learned with us. What follows are interviews with two very special individuals: James C. Hobby, executive vice president—global operations of SYKES Enterprises, and Dean Bruce, manager—retail sales improvement for the Ford Customer Service Division.

James C. Hobby, Executive Vice President—Global Operations, SYKES Enterprises

Jim Hobby has over 45,000 sales and service agents reporting up through global operations to his office in Tampa, Florida. Operating over 80 contact centers around the world, SYKES brings 30 years of expertise to every interaction. As the provider for many Fortune 500 companies, SYKES is trusted by industry leaders. Jim has served as the vice president of consumer care for Gateway and has held several senior management positions in customer care around the world with American Express Company and FedEx Corporation.

WGYH: Jim, with such a stellar background in what you do, how did you first get into the customer contact business?

HOBBY: I was at FedEx for many years, and I joined them as a senior financial analyst supporting the customer service division with the finance group. In those days, in order to get into management you had to go out and lead at the front line. So I ended up being a frontline manager in the call center for a year in Memphis. From there I moved all over the United States and Europe and ended up the director of customer operations for all of EMEA (Europe–Middle East–Africa). After that I went to American Express as their VP or head of operations, and from there I joined Gateway as VP of customer service. That's how I met John Sykes as a client, and I came to work for SYKES seven years ago.

WGYH: I didn't realize you lived so long in Europe.

HOBBY: Yes, a total of eight years, and now with SYKES for the last seven. I spend a lot of time on airplanes around the globe.

WGYH: When you look at 30-plus years in customer contact, what have the big trends been?

HOBBY: As I reflect back over the past 30 years, the top trends in change in call centers have all been technology-related. You don't see change in the fact that you still have to hire, train, motivate, and develop employees—the people aspect remained constant. With technology came the ability for what we call screen pops: matching agents with the requirements of a customer, interactive voice response to move phone calls around, and service or account information coming right up so the employee can focus more on helping you resolve an issue versus getting a whole lot of information that should already be there.

WGYH: If those are the trends in the last 30 years, I assume that technology will continue to be a key driver. What's coming?

HOBBY: It's already starting to happen, I mean, a great example of seeing change in the world was the use of social media in Cairo, Egypt. I think from a contact center perspective that we are going to see much more usage of social media like Facebook, with customer interactions actually transitioning from phone contact to social media.

WGYH: Really? We know a lot of people advocating that social media take the place of the cold call in sales. Ideally, how will social media play in customer service?

HOBBY: A great recent example that really hit home was in one of the recent snowstorms. Delta had a lot of stranded flights, and they actually had some of their phone agents log in to the Delta site for Twitter, and they were actually helping people get different reservation information on Twitter versus them having to call on the telephone. These people were able to access and get information even faster because the phone systems were so jammed, and you have the ability to service groups all at once, versus just individuals.

You also start to see companies hosting user groups and user forums so that if someone is having a problem, they just go in and ask, "Has anyone found the fix to . . ." whatever the issue is. Then you see expert users starting to come into the forums, and they are actually solving problems for people, and it isn't even with an employee of the company.

WGYH: Right, people will go to those maybe even before contacting the company.

HOBBY: Yeah, and it's real-time. One of the drawbacks even to e-mail has always been that people have to wait too long. A company might have a target to respond within 24 hours, but we have seen that a whole country can evolve in a day.

WGYH: When we look at some of these practices we've discussed, what drives them? Is it all cost-based?

HOBBY: I think it's a balance of saving and solving—meeting a customer's needs. At the end of the day, most customers want it solved as efficiently and as effectively as they can get it. So the faster you can get a resolution to a customer that works for *that* customer and that fixes an issue for them, the better they like it and the more loyalty you will get from that customer. That being said, in today's competitive environment, any services that you provide need to be as absolutely cost-effective as they can be.

WGYH: We talked a little bit earlier about the idea of service turning to sales. Your words [in an earlier meeting] stayed with us in reference to sales creeping into the service ranks of many organizations. You said, "It has gone from after-thought to overkill." We differentiate selling from service in terms of whose agenda is being addressed—shifting from the customers' agenda to our own. Why have organizations engaged in it?

HOBBY: I think through the years, as customer contact centers grew by hundreds of thousands of contacts at a time, companies' sales and marketing people started to see that with the DNC (*do not call*) list, phone marketing became harder and harder, direct mail contact was becoming more and more expensive, and when you had an existing base of people who were coming into you every day, it was logical that this could be a good mechanism for selling or up-selling.

With computers at Gateway, we discovered that some customers were calling in with a problem, and it was because they didn't have enough memory, or they wanted to play games, or they needed a flash drive. It wasn't a technical problem; they *needed* something. As they were having their problem, we actually found an opportunity to sell them something that would help resolve the issue that they were encountering. So it was having that ability to be able to take a problem or issue that a customer had and meeting that requirement.

That's where I think it's the most positive scenario. Like you mentioned with the airlines, if someone is getting on a flight, they might *like* to have a better seat offered to them. They might not want to sit in the middle in the back. To have the opportunity to actually add value to the customer when you offer it—that is an awesome sales opportunity.

WGYH: What is the difference between what you said—being able to provide a benefit and some value-add for someone—and perhaps a customer's perception that it's just one more way for them to charge me more?

HOBBY: That's when it becomes overkill. Where basically the customer sales and service agent has been told that we have "these eight items, and you offer every one until they take one, no matter what." Or if a customer is calling in and they are angry, they've had a very bad experience, and at the end of the call someone asks, "Oh, by the way, would you be interested in. . . ." I think we've all had those experiences where it feels the employee is just being forced to say something on the call versus listening, understanding needs, and offering something to the customer that's of benefit to them.

WGYH: For you, when does service become sales? When does service become selling?

HOBBY: For me service becomes selling when the service agent hears something that's needed from the customer calling in, and they know that there is something that they can sell them that will add value or help resolve the issue that the customer is calling in for.

WGYH: You have us thinking about the seamless integration of sales, marketing, and service. Does that ever get in the way—the problems inherent in sales and marketing taking over and running an operations group?

HOBBY: You know, it can get in the way, especially when a sales or marketing group hasn't done enough analysis or doesn't understand the customer base that's calling in. When they're not understanding or matching the products or offerings appropriately or when they then put the service employee in a position where they have to offer product X no matter what, that is when it becomes ineffective.

We have an analytics group that uses data gathering and Six Sigma methodologies to listen to phone calls. Sometimes their feedback is such that the offers are totally inappropriate in the way they are being positioned, and then we measure the conversion rates. Sometimes you find companies engaging in a sales pitch on a phone call—and they're getting a zero conversion rate or they're getting a conversion rate but then the cancellation rate is 90 percent. Nobody wins.

WGYH: Is that common? Are we finding that organizations are saying, "We need these people to sell more than we need them to service"? Is it simply that we need more of a return on their expense?

HOBBY: I do think that often the service part of a company is viewed as an expense. So the combination of service, sales, and marketing people will look for ways to generate revenue from the service side. Often managers take the view that sales and marketing are the revenue-generating part of the business and the servicing part of the business kind of becomes an afterthought.

WGYH: Just seen as overhead?

HOBBY: Yeah, seen as overhead. So trying to generate revenue; I support it. It's a positive thing to do in the right way. However, you can create just as much customer *dissatisfaction* as you can customer satisfaction if you just force revenue generation at the expense of other metrics.

WGYH: Okay, let's switch to the behavioral side, to the dialogue between agent and customer. What are the mistakes of the sales rookie or recruit? If you go to some of the habits that we have identified, which are the ones that *they* engage in?

HOBBY: As I mentioned, people in service are problem solvers, but at times they are so focused and narrow in their thinking that they seem to just stick to the script. You have a habit called propagandizing, and I believe it's something similar. When you're teaching someone they would follow a flow, with checklists, and you know, it takes a while to get so comfortable that they're thinking less about the script and the flow and more about how they are going to get to the resolution and probe with additional questions and information. For that reason I'm not a fan of doing up-sell or cross-sell with new employees in their first four to six months.

WGYH: How about people who maybe aren't new to it, people who have been a service provider for a fair amount of time, and now they're being asked to sell? What might the tendency be there?

HOBBY: Certainly, you are going to have some service people with the skills associated with sales, yet when I do focus groups with customer service agents and you mention the word "sell" to them, they just go into a panic and say, "No, no, no, I'm not a salesperson." At that point, you're asking them to go from solving a problem for someone to selling them something. There is a mindset in some people where they just don't like the concept that they have to sell something.

WGYH: The ones who do make that transition into selling, what skills do they have? What competencies do they have?

HOBBY: The people who struggle are the ones who have more of the technical view of the world. A precise view, so they tend to be much narrower in their thinking. A person capable of moving into service *and* sales has almost a caring capacity and an *interest in the customer,* not just to focus on resolving the issue that the customer calls in about. You have to be careful in that if your selling creates more work, more effort for them in the process, then you just undid what you gained. So it's being able to listen and probe and understand what the customer needs or desires, yet still making it easy for them to do business with you.

WGYH: Our premise is that stopping something is often easier and more powerful than trying to start something. What should someone *stop* doing in the process of service moving to sales?

HOBBY: Well, I think they should stop trying to put the sales effort in the same phone call or in the same amount of time that a service call used to take. Too often it becomes either too hurried or next to impossible to get it all done.

WGYH: For people who are moving from service into selling, what should they start doing or do more of?

HOBBY: They really should start listening to the needs of the customer versus just the issue that they have called in with—probing and listening to identify opportunities.

WGYH: Finally, a good service provider does a lot of things right in moving to sales. What should they continue doing?

HOBBY: They should continue having the caring attitude that most service people have for the customer. They tend to be in the job that they are in because they care about helping people and resolving issues for them.

WGYH: Jim, is there anything else that we're missing, any questions we didn't ask or thoughts that you have in terms of helping out those service-to-sales people?

HOBBY: You asked if any of the ineffective habits jumped out at me. Something that is so hard to get customer service people to do involves habit 12, never having to say you're sorry. Just getting them to apologize for the customer having that experience, not that that agent did anything wrong, just expressing that they are concerned and that they want to apologize for the experience they had. When you try to coach someone on basically apologizing or saying you're sorry, they are like, "But I didn't do anything." If I could pinpoint one habit to get over—to *give up*—it would be that. There is power in apology.

Dean Bruce, Manager—Retail Sales Improvement, Ford Customer Service Division

At one time, Ford and Lincoln Mercury dealership service departments saw 60 to 70 percent of their business come in from warranty and recall work. Today, Ford's quality is world-class and best in class. That's the good news. The bad news is that all that warranty work went away. Today the balance is reversed—60 to 70 percent of dealership service department revenue has to come from retail sales, not warranty claims; the service department has to move from service to sales. Dean Bruce is helping them make it happen.

Teaching credentials and 22 years of experience in the field with Ford Motor Company make Dean the right choice. Dean shared his insights into how Ford is making this move from service to sales.

WGYH: Can you give us a little of your background, Dean?

BRUCE: Years ago, I graduated with a bachelor's degree in business but went back to get my teaching credentials and taught for several years. That was what led me to the training area within Ford. I started with Ford in 1989 in the field organization. In Ford, you actually start in on the phones taking customer inquiries and then go out on the road and call on Ford and Lincoln dealerships. I've worked both the sales side, where you handle vehicle sales and distribution and product ordering, and the customer service side, where you focus on parts and service. I spent the better part of five years calling on dealers.

I then came up to Dearborn, and I have been doing retail improvement training, also first on the sales side of the dealership and now exclusively for the parts and service departments. Our go-to-market strategy for training is to identify the top performers by metrics—customer satisfaction, volume, gross, even market penetration—and then we go out and interview, mystery shop, and basically follow them around to understand exactly how they do their job. We then look at the average performers by the same criteria to see what they do and how they do it—and *closing that gap* is foundational to our mission. Our goal is to get them from average performance to top performance.

WGYH: Within the "back of the house"—the parts and service departments—what trends have you seen, and what do you see coming in the near future?

BRUCE: Okay, you go back maybe five to seven years, and Ford and Lincoln Mercury service repair facilities handled quite a bit of warranty work. We sold *lots* of cars. The car market itself was much bigger then, and we had a huge market share, and we want to try to say it nicely, but the quality wasn't at today's levels where we are best in class. So when you sell a lot of cars and you have some warranty issues, you fill your shops with warranty work. The dealers were geared for doing lots of warranty work. If you took a look at their overall business, it was probably 70 percent warranty, maybe 60 percent for the stores that were more retail-oriented, but yeah, it was 70 percent warranty and 30 percent retail business.

When I say retail, it's really the maintenance items, along with brakes, batteries, tires; that's how we break that up. So the dealers for the most part were really able to be service providers, because people would call in and say, "I need to come in; I have an issue with my vehicle," so it really wasn't difficult to fill the service department with warranty and scheduled maintenance.

Fast forward five to seven years later; now our quality is best in class, and we are at or above both Honda and Toyota, so dealers now do not have the warranty business base they used to have. Our dealers now run a very different service operation.

WGYH: How about the service advisors themselves? Are they generally, or were they generally, technicians or technically oriented folks at one time?

BRUCE: I think so, but not as many as you might think. You wouldn't want to paint everyone with a broad brush, but I would say they came either from technician ranks or more often from customer service backgrounds. That's really where they came up because you need to be personable, and you need to have thick skin, because customers aren't typically coming in for the fun of it. The critical piece for the advisor is they have got to get the information from the customer.

WGYH: Here's a two-part question for you. First, are service advisors now being asked to think in terms of selling and up-selling and cross-selling? And are they *compensated* now on the basis of what they sell? In other words, are they being rewarded and incentivized for sales?

BRUCE: I believe so, yes. I think that has really shifted as well. It was probably more customer satisfaction 5 to 10 years ago, where now it's customer satisfaction *along with sales*. The company has initiatives and incentives to drive revenue in the service and parts departments too. We have incentives throughout the year where we reward advisors who sell brakes, batteries, tires—and we look at both parts sales and penetration. We certainly encourage that, and the dealers are doing that more as well. I think you'll find that if you take 10 dealers, 8 or even 9 of them heavily incentivize their advisors on what they sell.

WGYH: These are the trends in selling. What is different from the customers' point of view? What has changed in buying?

BRUCE: Well, I think for the customer, we have some barriers to overcome. Customers like us for technical expertise and original equipment parts. On the other hand, there exists a perception that a dealership can be inconvenient and expensive. Those are *significant* obstacles that are a result of the competitive options that consumers have today versus 10 or 20 years ago.

WGYH: Let's shift our thinking now to the people involved. You have professionals who at one time were service providers, period, and now feel the pressure to sell. What makes a veteran or a rookie different in that environment?

BRUCE: I think that the effective vet is really an advocate for the customer. Our research tells us that the customer wants more than anything for the service department to value their time and to feel in control of the situation. The veteran puts the customer in control, and by "in control" I mean that they inform the customers and then give them options. From a systems perspective, the key is first of all an appointment so that when the customer comes in, they aren't lined up 10 deep waiting for an advisor. Time is a significant differentiator for customers—be efficient and don't waste their time but allow enough for effective interactions. One of the ways we do that is through our "Multi-Point Inspection Report Card." Our most experienced service advisors do this multipoint inspection on every vehicle, on every visit, and it builds trust. It gives a green, yellow, red designation of condition to all the systems on the vehicle, and the technician even takes a deep look at the vehicle while it's up on the lift: pull the tires, look at brake depths and pads, and things like that—tire treads, you name it. The technician notes any issues with the vehicle. This allows the advisor to be an advocate, to be a pro. Sometimes I think "pro" can be short for "process."

WGYH: Right now, let's take a look at a few of the ineffective habits, and if you would, tell us if it would be more likely to be committed by a vet or by a rookie or draftee. Selling past the close—the irresistible urge to verbalize, execute every step in the process. Veteran or rookie?

BRUCE: While you can have someone who's been around 10 years be just as ineffective as a newbie, for the most part that is more of a rookie mistake. A pro, somebody who really gets it, gives their customer the options, and then allows the customer to make the decision. I think on the other side, a rookie can be nervous and talk right through the sale. With that in mind, I would say selling past the close is a rookie mistake.

WGYH: How about curb qualifying—the tendency to judge a prospect superficially from a distance?

BRUCE: That one I don't think happens as much in service, but if someone were to do it, it would be the veteran—the one who's seen it all. I think the veteran might see an older vehicle and assume the customer can't afford a particular repair and not even suggest it for that reason.

WGYH: How about vocal filler—the overuse of unnecessary and meaningless verbal qualifiers?

BRUCE: I've got to say that it would be the rookie who maybe wouldn't have their questioning process down. I think you hit two points, though. The "umm," "uhh," and just kind of rambling—that's the rookie. The ineffective habit of the vet would be repeating the likes of "I'm going to be honest with you here now." It makes you wonder what they've been lying about up until that point.

WGYH: Exactly. Another habit is one-upping—the constant need to top our conversational partner.

BRUCE: Yeah, that's a veteran mistake, although I'm not sure that is as common yet in a service-to-sales environment. In my experience, it could happen more up in the sales department, the same as your habit of using tension in sales would be another that might happen more often in the sales department. Yet, the opportunity is there now in the service department. I can hear the veteran saying, "Hey, if you don't get these tires fixed, you could have a blowout."

WGYH: With the enthusiasm you communicate when talking about your efforts to grow retailer revenue, how about the habit of withholding passion or energy?

BRUCE: Yes, for *every* customer coming in, it's important to them, you have to have the same kind of commitment, passion, and advocacy for that customer, each and every customer, every time—and I think that habit is more often a veteran trait. It's just that they have seen *so* many vehicles, *so* many people, that they lose their rookie enthusiasm. I don't believe there's any intent to shortchange the customer—it's just such a high-energy business. Those outside of sales often can't relate.

WGYH: How about one last one, Dean, which we call throwing others under the bus—rookie or veteran?

BRUCE: Again, the opportunity is there for that to occur in our service business, and it's most likely a rookie mistake, especially when there is pressure to sell. But while there are so many variables in service—parts, shop and technician scheduling, simply fulfilling the promises of others—those dealers that have learned to focus on the customer have been able to eliminate this habit.

So What? What did you learn?

- When service turned to sales, it was thought to be salvation.
- Relevant trends in service turning to sales: technology and the evolution of communication, economics, "service" as a cost center
- The power of mindset: Are we setting ourselves up for failure?

■ Habits that a draftee might fall into: vocal filler, selling past the close, explaining failure, never having to say you're sorry, throwing others under the bus, propagandizing

Now What? What might you do now?

■ Talk to your boss about this service-to-sales shift. What is his perspective on the utility and applicability in your world?

■ What about you? Does the power of mindset work for you or against you (be honest)?

■ If you are in sales and don't want to be, what can you do to improve your mindset?

How to Choose What to Stop

9

Take a deep breath again . . . let it out. It is time. You've studied the habits, and you've considered them through the filters of the different demographics: veterans, rookies, draftees, and the pros we all strive to be. It's time now to choose what to stop—what to give up for your customers. We often say that to be more effective you don't have to do a lot, but you have to do *something*.

Let's take a few minutes to understand the nature of the task at hand and some of the dynamics that are in play.

First, let's narrow it down. Very few of us are capable of losing weight, stopping smoking, getting fit, and starting a new job all at the same time. This holds true for just about any attempt at behavioral change. As we've said, most of us are busier than we have ever been in our lives; we're over-solicited, over-committed, and at times overwhelmed.

Let's simplify by learning from the U.S. Marines and taking advantage of the power of the triad—nothing more than threes. When it comes to choosing something to change about you, something to *stop* doing, pick no more than three habits to consider. Thus, your first challenge becomes one of narrowing a list of 16 down to a list of 3.

INFORMATION AND EMOTION

As you read through Chapter 6 we are guessing that there were a few habits that you recognized as something you do a little of or a lot of. Some of you might even be fortunate enough to be able to acknowledge a single habit right off, a habit staring you right in the face that if eliminated would make your life and the lives of those around you far more effective.

We are betting, though, that there are even more of you who either recognize a significant segment of the habits as something others you know would engage in (right down to putting names instead of numbers on the habits) or who personally identify with so many of the habits that it's difficult to decide where to start.

As we found in helping leaders figure out what to stop doing in order to to maintain empathy with their people, the bad habits in sales fall under two conceptual umbrellas: information and emotion. Go back and take a look at all 16 habits and you'll find that practitioners of any of them suffer from a serious overload or underload of information or emotion.

It is not that information and emotion themselves are the culprit; they aren't good or bad in and of themselves. It is in providing the *appropriate amount* of information or emotion that we maintain empathy or destroy it.

Let's start with information. The destructive habit of selling past the close is a case of *way too much* information. The customer is ready to buy, ready to end the transaction, and what does the guilty party do? Share some more. Several of the ineffective habits revolve around TMI (too much information): vocal filler, one-upping, and explaining failure, to name a few.

The flip side of the information mismatch is that when we aren't providing too much, we're *gathering too little*. Curb qualifying, selective hearing, and propagandizing are shining examples that revolve around too little information (TLI). In each case the salesperson suffers from what has come to be known as *premature elaboration*—gather just a little bit of data and we're off and running on our script.

Thus, some of us suffer (and therefore our customers suffer) the effects of information abuse. But, what about emotion? How does that come into play? If you think back to other ineffective habits covered in Chapter 6 with-holding passion, never having to say you're sorry, using tension as a tool, and even over-familiarity—an emotional mismatch is what destroys the empathic connection here.

Invest too little emotion, and you come across as disinterested, cold, or uncaring. No one wants to do business with someone who can't maintain his or her own excitement level (let alone create a little contagious enthusiasm). But inject too much emotion, and tension abounds. How do you respond when met with pressure to buy, manufactured deadlines, or elevated tempers in a business setting? We're guessing with either fight or flight, and neither one is conducive to lasting rapport.

A good starting point is to look inward. When you have difficulties with interpersonal communication, do they usually revolve around the dynamics of information (TMI *or* TLI), or do they result from an emotional spring-load? Which one tends to trip you up, information or emotion? Usually, people know intuitively where they tend to err, and this determination can give you a good head start on focusing on which habit might be the one to tackle.

GATHERING DATA

If at this point you feel you know just what to stop to make your customer interactions more effective, good for you. The next couple of paragraphs will confirm your diagnosis. If you're still not sure which habit is your highest-payout interpersonal fault, these tips on gathering data should be just what you need. Here are four ways in which you can collect information about yourself, par-ticularly about how you come across to others.

Casual Remarks

What "casual" remarks do others use when they talk about you? When others speak about you—or to you—what do they say? As conscious human beings we are constantly noticing what others look like, what they wear, what they say, how they say it, and to whom they say it.

What we would suggest you do now is *notice with purpose*. Notice what people say about you. Notice (and remember) what kind of tone your customers use in conversing with you. It can teach you a great deal. We guarantee that if you become a skilled noticer of others, patterns will emerge.

Write down a list of comments you hear over just a day or two and rate them as simply positive or negative—write nothing more complex than that. What do they tend to be about? What comments come up over and over again? Is it, "Ray, you seem to be in a hurry for this contract" or "Do we have to move on that right now?" The question to answer is, Has a pattern emerged? Are you hearing the same types of comments from several people or on several occasions?

Keep at the list of the remarks you hear for a day or a week—as long as it takes for an offending habit to become clear to you. Your customers or loved ones won't know what you're up to, and you will be gathering powerful data in your search for what to stop with those you care about.

The Mute Button

We know there are plenty of times you've wanted to do this. We know there are certain situations in which you'd love to have a real-time mute button to press (or maybe even a fast-forward button). Agreed, it would make some days a lot easier. In fact, you *have* the ability to tune out the words that others are using (some of us have gotten pretty good at it) and focus solely on nonverbal communication, only this time you can do it with purpose.

One activity we use in our training involves asking participants to pretend they're watching a movie with the sound off. We ask them to notice physical movement and the positioning of others. We ask them to notice facial expression, proximity (the personal distance they establish and maintain), eye contact, and other indicators of interpersonal ease or discomfort.

Finally, we ask the participants to consider how they factor into the muted display. What part did they play in the silent movie? Do others appear to become more or less comfortable when interacting with them? Do others move closer upon their approach or farther away? Do others seek eye contact, or do they avert their eyes? These are the questions to ask yourself when you're able to observe others around you "with the sound off."

Using your own personal mute button, you can make a call as to whether you attract or repel those around you. Then you can zero in on just what you seem to be doing to create the attraction or separation. By noticing with purpose, you can discover what to do—and what not to do—to allow you to begin to *act* with purpose. Premeditated action (or inaction) is the end target we'll be searching for in future chapters.

Your Casual Remarks

With this technique we are again asking you to become what a close friend and colleague, Dr. Warren Bennis, would call a "first-class noticer." This time, however, you're leaving others muted and turning up the volume on your own monologue. What are you saying about you? Whether self-deprecating or self-aggrandizing, how would you describe the patterns that emerge around what you say about yourself?

As vocal filler or for who knows what reason, you might notice that you often preface conversations with something like "I really mean this, Sarah" or "I'm not going to kid you, Kate." If this is the case, what might it mean? Does it mean you regularly *don't* mean what you say? We don't think so. Could it be confusing to a customer as they try to understand you? Perhaps.

At times what we say about ourselves reveals with brutal honesty exactly what we believe and feel. At other times, it may represent the exact opposite of what we believe to be true. These are habits of human nature—to sometimes mask and sometimes highlight our strengths and weaknesses. What we want for you is self-knowledge. Through self-knowledge you can begin to premeditate effective behavior.

Homework

Do you believe that your ineffective habits on the job magically disappear when you hit the front door? It's highly unlikely. If your interpersonal challenges at work stem from emotion-level mismatches, you can bet that issues you have with your spouse, significant other, or children most often result from failings of emotional intelligence as well. Those who over-inform their customers probably have heard some approximation of "Okay, I get the message" from a loved one as well.

We've coached hundreds of individuals who are living testimony to the idea that perhaps some of your best guidance on what to do or not do to be more effective at work comes from those you live with. Our suggestion here is that you show the list of habits (just the habit overviews) to your husband, wife, or other person of interest and ask that person to pick one habit you are most guilty of and one habit you are least guilty of.

You might even select three people outside your workplace to provide you with this insight. Compare their perspectives with your suspicions. We're hoping you will find their selections aligned with your own. In any case, we are going to steal a point of order from the Feed*Forward* process coming up in Chapter 11. In asking someone for his or her perspective, all you are allowed to say in response to the input is "thank you." No judgment, rebuttal, discussion, or dismissal—just "thank you." Tell that person that you appreciate his or her taking the time to help you and that you will keep him or her posted. What you are trying to do right now is gather data; *using* the data comes next.

CHOOSING A BEHAVIOR

You have done your homework. You have reached out to those around you personally and perhaps professionally too. You have dialed up your sensitivity to others and your own voice through targeted noticing. By now you should have at least narrowed your search for what to stop doing with your customers.

We're hoping you may have even discovered some new motivators in the process. What next, then? *Selecting a behavior.* It's time to choose what ineffective habit you would like to curb in relating to others.

In setting yourself up for success in a final selection of a habit to work on, there are two key concepts to keep in mind: *because of versus in spite of* and *the laws of energy.*

Because Of versus In Spite Of

We think that people in the sales profession are uniquely susceptible to confusing these concepts in that salespeople tend to receive the acknowledgment of performance (read, sales reports) and the reinforcement of their achievement (read, commissions, incentives, bonuses, or spiffs) on a constant basis.

Whether on a quarterly, monthly, weekly, or even daily basis, salespeople receive data and rewards at a far more hectic pace than that experienced by their staff counterparts.

In itself, this isn't bad. This pay for performance approach is fine as long as everyone is associating the same behaviors with the rewards provided. Problems arise when we associate the rewards received with the wrong behaviors, when we confuse correlation with causality.

We mistakenly believe that we receive an organizational reward *because of* certain things that we did. Perhaps we pressured the client, poached the lead, or played a little loose with the truth to create a sense of urgency with the customer. In fact, we have received the rewards *in spite of* the behaviors we've engaged in. Confusing correlation with causality is simply a matter of mixing up because of and in spite of.

Let's face it. You are a successful professional because you do a lot of the right things and you do a lot of things right. In selecting an area of focus for behavioral change, make sure you understand that it is not your because-of list that we're interested in right now. Your in-spite-of list is where you will find what to stop doing to maintain rapport and empathy.

The Laws of Energy

What we know from the physical world we can apply to the behavioral world. Many years ago Kurt Lewin's theories on the process of successful behavioral change were summarized through the analogy of "unfreezing," "trial," and "refreezing." The theory is that we seem to be *frozen* into set patterns of behavior. As with changing the shape of a block of ice, to create a different behavior pattern we need to unfreeze it, put it into a different form, and then refreeze it. Let's see what we can learn through this analogy from the laws of energy.

What does it take to change the state of water from solid to liquid? Heat. Simple enough. In the physical sciences we know that it ultimately takes a specific number of calories, a specific amount of heat, to change the state of a gram of water from solid to liquid. And how do we produce heat? Energy.

It takes a lot of *energy* to "unfreeze" water, to change it from a solid to a liquid state. The parallel to our behavioral world is that here, as in the world of physics, *change takes energy.* To unfreeze our behaviors, to stop engaging in what we have come to rely on unconsciously when interacting with others, we need to expend tremendous amounts of energy.

Our message to you is to make sure that the change you ultimately select is one in which you can access a tremendous amount of personal energy to make it happen. It simply can't be change that your boss wants you to make or your spouse or significant other wants you to make; it has to be a felt need to change that *you* possess, no one else. You must possess the energy in reference to the change; you're going to need it.

We mentioned earlier that together the three of us have 100 years of experience in the behavioral sciences. Ironically, among the three of us we carry some 100 years of first-marriage relationship experience as well. In all our 100 years of firsthand data around the process of behavioral change in the world of marital relationships, rarely has significant change come about because the spouse wanted the other person to change. The need for change—the energy required for change—must come from within.

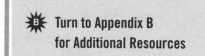

B Turn to Appendix B
for Additional Resources

HOW TO CHOOSE WHAT TO STOP

You started by understanding the task at hand. You sorted your thinking on the basis of informational dynamics versus emotional. You have become a first-class noticer of what you and others think about you both at work and at home. You have double-checked your thinking to find your in-spite-of behaviors. Finally, you've applied the laws of physics and energy to ensure that the behaviors you decide to stop are your behaviors—what you want to work on eliminating.

Stay with us; the journey has begun. Next stop: *how to get from here . . . to there.*

So What? What did you learn?

- The power of the triad
- Sorting by information versus emotion
- Casual remarks—theirs and yours. What do they say?
- The "mute" button at work and at home
- Because of versus in spite of and the laws of energy

Now What? What might you do now?

- Pick one habit and get ready to attack it until it doesn't matter anymore. Record the habit you select to give up in Appendix B.
- Begin to let those who matter to you know what you've chosen (don't be bashful).
- Get ready to move from here . . . to there.

How to Get From Here . . . to There

The special process of change for successful salespeople and a guide to getting help, getting ideas, and getting there.

- Dig more deeply into the success delusion to understand assumptions about oneself and why change is different for successful people.
- Learn and internalize the concept of self-selection and the enablers of change for successful people.
- Undertake the development of a team of helpers in the process of interpersonal change to rate, suggest, participate, and change *with* you.
- Master the art and practice of Feed*Forward* as a tool for generating ideas for change.
- Understand and establish a mechanism for follow-up to ensure lasting positive behavioral change

The Rules Are Different for You: Successful Salespeople and Change

10

First, let's be clear: This book is not for the troubled, the failing, or the "broken" salesperson. This is all about change for *successful* salespeople, and the rules of change are different for successful people. When you are new to the job and focused on the basics of acquiring product knowledge and mastering the functional aspects, the study of the human interface should wait. Along the same lines, when your sales are last on the team and your job is on the line, external forces will provide the inspiration to try new approaches—*or else*.

Our focus is on helping successful salespeople become even better. Whether you're in the middle of the pack or one of the 20 percent who often turn in the lion's share of a team's revenue, we're targeting those of you who want to improve and take it to the next level. The old saying "If it ain't broke, don't fix it" doesn't apply to helping successful people change. Why would a top golfer, after winning a major tournament, completely retool his swing? Why would a great football team, after winning a championship, replace half a dozen key players? The laws of physics state that it takes a lot of energy for anyone to change. Our coaching practice of over 20 years tells us that not everyone can change.

You might ask, Can we identify up front the candidates who are most likely to get better? As it turns out, yes, we can. Interestingly, it has nothing to do with intelligence; all of you reading this work are smart and well educated. It also rarely has anything to do with personality; over the years we have worked with virtually every type. Introverts may listen better than extroverts, but extroverts may be more self-aware. Some personality types have more of a natural ability to develop and follow a behavioral action plan than do others. Understanding personality is helpful. In the end, however, no personality type is more likely than another to be a successful candidate for personal change.

WHAT DOES MAKE A DIFFERENCE?

What we found does make a difference in behavioral change is that an individual *owns the developmental issue* and *is motivated to change it*. It takes both. First, let's look at owning the issue. In our interviews for this book we talked with dozens of sales managers. One of the questions we asked was, "What is it about average sales representatives that keeps them from rising to a higher level?" We got a variety of answer patterns, such as inability to empathize with the customer, asking inappropriate questions, and not listening effectively—these things all ended up in the 16 habits. What stuck out like a sore thumb for us came up when we asked, "How does the average sales rep *react* when this is pointed out?" Almost without exception, we heard: "They defend to the death what they are doing."

Responses to negative performance feedback varied from "Look how we turned out at Acme Chemical" to "What about the great success we've had with ABC Beverage?" The salespeople tended to defend or excuse their ineffective behaviors: "You just caught me on a bad day," "That was the exception," "I don't usually do that," "As a matter of fact, you're being picky by even bringing it up." Or they *justify* their behaviors: "Because of my in-depth knowledge of the customer . . . with the competition in this market . . . due to tight budgets— I *had* to do this." Sometimes we even got the infamous "It's not me—it is the *customer,* who would try anyone's patience." You get the picture. In all these cases the root cause lies within the sales representative in that he or she doesn't own the issue. He or she defends it, excuses it, justifies it, or, if nothing else works, lays blame for it.

CHANGE = DISSATISFACTION > RESISTANCE

Although we know that change will occur whenever dissatisfaction is greater than resistance, a question we often hear is, "Can you teach an old dog new tricks?" You bet you can. We have examples of people effecting significant change even in the later stages of their careers. Age has nothing to do with it. Nor is it about personality or intelligence. The first step in change for successful individuals is to own it, to recognize that the issue isn't about the customer, the market, or even the product—it is about you.

Second, you have to want to change. Simply being aware that you "add too much value" or "make excuses" isn't enough. To summon up the energy to change, you have to be highly motivated to make the change, and often motivation comes from anticipated pain (read, dissatisfaction) as much as anything else. One of our overseas affiliates once said, "Pleasure motivates, but pain gets you to move arse."

Think of people trying to quit smoking. It's easy to understand why one should quit. It is horribly expensive and awful for people's health. There is even a very straightforward plan to quitting—just stop smoking. Don't buy them, borrow them, or put one in your mouth—just stop. But as anyone who has ever done it realizes, it is not easy. Our dissatisfaction with the status quo has to be greater than our inherent resistance to change or change will never take place.

This is difficult for salespeople who have been successful on the job for a few years. They believe in themselves. They have to—it's part of the job. They're not dissatisfied with how things are going. They believe they have the talent and skills to win the game and keep on winning. We call this the *success delusion.* Under this delusion we tend to kid ourselves about our accomplishments and what actually created success. We overestimate our contributions, have an elevated opinion of our professional skills, and conveniently forget any low points. This delusion grows out of four key beliefs that are common to almost all successful salespeople:

- I *have* succeeded.
- I *can* succeed.
- I *will* succeed.
- I *choose* to succeed.

I HAVE/I CAN/I WILL/I CHOOSE

With a visceral conviction that *I have succeeded* in the past, successful salespeople generally have loads of confidence in their skills and abilities, sometimes well founded and sometimes not so much. Either way, what stories will you hear them repeating? Will you get recounts of their abject failures, a retelling of their competitive losses? Not likely. What you will hear is a highlight reel of their competitive conquests and heroic efforts in successfully pulling off the impossible against all odds. Their recollection of the past is edited unconsciously to amp up the bright spots and filter out the dim. How else can we get up in the morning to face others in a profession that by design includes a comparatively high percentage of rejection, failure, and second-place finishes?

In the sales world we get lots of positive reinforcement for success, all contributing to the confidence displayed in the belief "I can succeed." There are awards, trophies, and letters from senior management congratulating us on our success. And what kind of feedback do salespeople get when results are average? Why, none, of course. That's why we remember the successes. We place the winning plaque on the wall in the office for all to see. The letters are saved in a special file that we like to read from time to time. It is little wonder that the success lives on and the rest is forgotten.

It is this rock-solid belief that we have succeeded in the past—and the innate confidence that we will succeed in the future—that generates the delusion paradox. The same beliefs that help us become successful can make change—specifically the motivation to change—really difficult. On the one hand, the belief provides the ability to ignore the odds against a particular sale.

On the other hand, this overestimation of our prowess keeps us from realizing it's time to make a change.

Are you thinking, "This doesn't happen to me; I'm more realistic than that"? The good news is that salespeople are less likely than others to grossly overrate their contributions. The bad news is that they still overrate themselves. In all the work we have done—all over the world with over 50,000 participants—we ask people to answer the following question: "How would you compare your performance on the job with a group you would consider your professional peers?" In general we find that 80 percent of people rate themselves in the top 20 percent of their peer group and 50 percent rate themselves in the top 10 percent. Globally, we carry a pretty high opinion of ourselves.

Some professions, such as physicians, pilots, and those in law enforcement, rate themselves even higher, with 90 percent placing themselves in the top 10 percent. Two other professions, however—salespeople and professional athletes—tend to rate themselves more conservatively and perhaps more accurately: More like only 30 percent place themselves in the top 10 percent. What do these two groups have in common that the others don't? Consistent, objective measurement of performance.

Professional athletes get statistics on every area of their performance. Professional golfers know how many times they hit the fairway on their tee shots and how many putts they take per hole. Tennis professionals keep track of aces, unforced errors, and points at the net. Athletes in team sports have their statistics compared to those of everyone else at their position, not just on their club. If you are a forward for the Los Angeles Lakers, your statistics are compared not only to those of other Lakers; your rebounds, free throws, and assists are compared to those of every forward in professional basketball, both past and present. Professional salespeople live in the same data-driven world.

The last belief is "I choose to succeed." Unlike people in other professions, who may be victims of random circumstance, successful salespeople believe that we are doing what we are doing by personal choice. We have a high need for *self*-determination. We want to do things our way and hate being told what do or, even worse, how to do it. It is this belief in ourselves and in the choices we make that breeds our commitment. It's often our decision when to begin our day, how to organize our time, how to sequence our calls, and how to adapt our presentations to specific customer needs.

Like all important life choices, choosing to succeed can be a positive, integral part of our success. This personal commitment has a high correlation with achievement in virtually every field, and it enables us to stay the course when the going gets tough. On the downside, when people believe that their success is a result of their choices, it is not easy to "choose" change. The more success we have enjoyed, the more likely we are to have a firm commitment to and belief in ourselves. The more we believe that our behavior is a result of our own choices, the more difficult it is to decide to change.

UNDERSTANDING NATURAL LAW

We've come to the point of knowing what habit to stop and being aware of some of the beliefs that might get in our way. How do we know what will move us to make a change rather than be another empty resolution? Let's take a look at natural law.

One of the humbling realities we have discovered in our coaching practice is that *we* aren't going to change anyone. It is up to each individual. In more than a hundred years' combined experience at working with people to help them become more successful, we have observed only one reason people ever change. They obey natural law, which is defined as follows:

> **Natural Law: People will do something—including changing their behavior—only if it can be demonstrated that doing so is in their own best interest, as defined by their own values.**

At the end of the day, people do what they perceive to be in their own best interests. It governs every choice and decision. We ask, What is in it for me?

Why would a top performer sacrifice personal gain to help the sales team? Perhaps because there is something else in it for her (promotion, respect, admiration of peers). Why would someone turn down a job offer for more money? Because he has decided that the extra money is not worth it; he enjoys the team he is on now. It wouldn't make him happier to earn more.

Natural law is the reason people quit high-paying jobs to do something completely different. Recently we worked with a high-level sales executive who quit his job to work with a nonprofit firm. In an effort to keep him, his company offered him even more money. He readily responded, "It's not about the money; it is about what I want to do with my life."

As was discussed earlier, successful salespeople often have little reason to change what they are doing. Past behavior has brought them recognition and a sense of accomplishment. Why not stick with what has worked?

Most people's resistance to change can be overcome only by appealing to natural law. Everyone has a hot button that can be pushed, and that hot button is self-interest. It isn't the same for all people. Now is the time to take a deep breath and take another look at *you*. Take a look around yourself. Sales is a difficult and competitive career. It can be stressful and lonely. Why do you do it? What keeps you coming back day after day? Why do you do what you do?

If you probe deeper (and we have) to identify the motives that move you to take risks, change what you are doing, or change the way you are doing it, it usually comes down to four factors: *money, power, status,* and *relationships*. These are the payoffs to change. The hot button is different for each person and often evolves over time, but it is always guided by self-interest. Let's look at them in turn.

Money

When considered in reference to salespeople, money probably embodies the most commonly held paradigm of external motivation within organizations. Most believe that money motivates—and it does up to a point. Most sales compensation plans are designed to pay more money for more performance, but is that the primary motivator? How does it work in reference to natural law? What need does it fill?

Abraham Maslow's hierarchy of needs states that motivators of behavior start at the bottom of a pyramid, beginning with satisfying basic requirements for food and shelter. If you don't have those things, you will be motivated to work to achieve them (and not terribly interested in too much else until you get them). Once you have them, however, they no longer drive your behavior.

As you satisfy each lower-level need, you move up to satisfy subsequent levels of safety needs, social needs, and things such as recognition and achievement. Money is a powerful stimulus at several lower levels through the process and can be a great scorecard to measure the competitive nature of many salespeople at moderate to high levels. But does it motivate all of us, and for how long?

A few years ago, working with a medical device company that would be considered top of the food chain in sales, we found the average sales representative earned well into a six-figure income (and the top earners even more). When we interviewed one of the sales managers, he lamented that motivation was a significant issue even within this highly paid group.

He went on to explain, "I feel like I'm the manager of the New York Yankees. Everyone on the team makes an incredible amount of money. When they first join the team, it is like being called up from the minor leagues. They are highly motivated and feel honored to be here. After a few years, however, there is a change. They get comfortable in the job. The money doesn't seem like so much anymore. In fact, some almost feel an entitlement in reference to their compensation: 'I'm a major league player, and that's what we make in the big leagues.'"

As we have all seen, there are major league players who jog to first base on a fly ball. They stop hustling, stop giving it 110 percent. Offering an additional $10,000 won't make a difference when people are already earning more money than they ever dreamed possible. Money can lead to more dissatisfaction than satisfaction in the sales motivation equation (do we sense agreement?). So what becomes the hot button? There must be something else.

Power

Power, along with the organizational freedom it often gives those who have it, can be a significant motivator. Are you tired of driving around town every day looking for a parking place, talking with the same people, doing your own administrative work? Everyone comes to you with requests or blame. The people in marketing need this, and the people in accounting need that. The customer makes demands.

Sales does have its rewards, but you went to college to do more than this. Bottom line: There are people who will put in tremendous amounts of extra effort and personal sacrifice to get promoted. Sometimes those promoted end up earning less than they did in line sales but choose management for other reasons. Is that your hot button? There's nothing inherently positive or negative (or necessarily important) in the influence potential that power brings—only the motivational effect it has on you is important.

Status

Status is closely related to power, but status doesn't always have to entail a promotion. In fact there are people who have no interest in the trappings of management. They are, however, very conscience of status. Who gets recognized and who doesn't? How are they referred to when introduced by others? Many organizations have a special elite group of "the best" salespeople who earn special status. And they can get (and desire) the trappings of the status: better company cars, a different title on business cards, award trips.

One salesperson we interviewed began his career in sales at Johnson & Johnson. At that time there was a special club of achievement called the "ring club." It was based on cumulative sales performance, which was recognized with a special gold ring. The number that had to be reached was so big that it could not be achieved in a single year. The J&J rep recently had attended a reunion of people who all started their careers in sales at Johnson & Johnson many years earlier. Some of those people had moved on to other organizations. One was president of his own company, and several were VPs in large multinationals. One thing everyone noticed was that all those years later, they all wore their rings to the reunion. As evidenced by that small sign of recognized status, the pride was still there.

Relationships

As a driver of behavior, relationships are not just about being popular. As much as most of us want to be liked, it goes beyond that. Some people come to realize they just don't want to spend their lives working in a solitary environment. They want to work as part of a team. They want to know at the end of the day that they have made a difference. The draw of affiliation is a powerful pull.

One of our partners recently interviewed retired managers. One of the questions he asked was, "What do you take the most pride in during your career?" These were people who lived through mergers, acquisitions, and dramatic new product innovations. Surprisingly, the most common answer involved relationships with people on the team. It sounded something like this: "When Natalie and I first began working together, she couldn't tell you the difference between sales and marketing. Today she is VP of sales and marketing and is doing a wonderful job. I'm proud of her." Does making a difference in other people's lives mean something special to you?

If you know what matters to you, it is easier to commit to change. If you cannot readily identify what matters, you won't know when it is threatened or when an opportunity arises. *People change their ways when something they truly value is offered or threatened. It is natural law!* Take the time to consider what might motivate you to change. Take the time to inventory the drivers that might help you stop the ineffective habits you have chosen. Put natural law on your side.

Stay with us. Now you know what special challenges you face as a successful salesperson trying to improve. Coming up are the three steps that let you do it actively and effectively.

So What? What did you learn?

- Self-selected change and self-selected raters
- Change = dissatisfaction > resistance
- The "success delusion": I have, I can, I will, I choose to succeed
- Understanding natural law: money, power, status, relationships

Now What? What might you do now?

- Get ready to change. Ask yourself, Do I want to change?
- Assess your motives. What payoff do you strive for?
- Make a mental list of those you want to involve in your change.

Getting Help, Getting Ideas, Getting There

11

Through experience we know that for a successful salesperson there are three steps in the process of achieving positive, measurable behavioral change:

- **Getting help.** You can't do it alone. Recruiting stakeholders makes it possible to overcome the success delusion.
- **Getting ideas.** It is necessary to practice what we call Feed*Forward* to look to the future and not the past.
- **Getting there.** You must have a follow-up process to make your efforts more than an event, more than intent.

To kick the chapter off, let's focus on what it means and what it takes to get the help you need to change—for good.

GETTING HELP: RECRUITING STAKEHOLDERS

Behavioral change is not something you do alone. It requires two people: one to change and one to notice it. It is this personal acknowledgment of change requiring the involvement of someone other than oneself that makes it obvious (and imperative) that a person get help. We all need help in planning the change, providing suggestions for improvement strategies and tactics, and letting us know when we get there.

This step requires that you *talk* with people. You have to tell people what you plan to do. This is the point at which some (in fact, a lot) of people resist. They ask, "Why do I need to go around telling everyone what I'm going to do? It takes time. I'm not convinced there is any good purpose for it. And to be honest, it is potentially a little embarrassing. After all, if I work at this and improve, isn't that the bottom line? Isn't that what matters?"

Changing Perception

There is perception, and then there is reality. Which do you want to change? Both, of course. You want to improve, and you want people to see the improvement and appreciate the new you, which is part of becoming more effective. Which do you think is more difficult to change, perception or reality? Interestingly, it is far more difficult to change perception.

There is a concept in psychology called cognitive dissonance. It says that we view people in a manner that is consistent with our existing stereotypes (positive or negative). If you are seen as someone who is consistently selective in your hearing—a person unaccustomed to listening effectively—everything you do will be filtered through the image that others have of you. Even when you do engage, keep quiet, ask for clarification, and respond appropriately, others will see that as an exception to the rule. You are still a selective listener to them. With this going on, it can seem next to impossible for people to see you as improving. We tell our clients that with the cognitive dissonance factor in play, you have to improve 100 percent to get 10 percent credit.

Advertising

The odds improve considerably, however, if you tell people that you are trying to change and are very specific about the area you want to improve. Now your efforts are on their radar screen. When your company introduces a new product, do they advertise? Of course they do. You have to get the message out to the buying public: "Hey, I've got something new, something I think you will like." Even the smallest mom-and-pop retail store will at least put up a sign, and major corporations plan entire campaigns to advertise the NEW. That is what you need to do—advertise. Tell the people who you want to notice exactly what it is they should notice.

Once isn't enough. We've already mentioned the concept of multi-touch marketing. We've known for a long time that it takes several touches to create awareness, interest, and acceptance in the buying public. The same holds true in your campaign for change. Be prepared as well for some of those important to you to say, "I don't think this is a problem for you." That is okay. In fact, no matter what you select for improvement, from experience we can almost guarantee that someone (the customer who loves you, a peer you've known a long time) won't see what you've selected to stop as a significant area of improvement for you.

What you don't want to say at this point is, "You are wrong—I do need to improve." You might leave these people thinking, "Gee, I thought Susan was pretty effective, but I must have been wrong. I guess she really does have some problems." A better response would be, "I didn't say I was awful, just that I'd like to do better. As part of my personal development plan this is something I'd like to improve." If you respond this way, what might these people think? We have researched this response hundreds of times, and they are much more likely in this case to say, "As good as Susan is now, she is still working to improve and get even better. I respect that." That's the response we want, don't you think?

The first step is to advertise the new you to everyone who will listen. Remember, you aren't running a one-day sale here. You are trying to create a lasting change; it's a long-term campaign. Don't assume that people will hear your message the first or second time you deliver it. Advertising means repeating it over and over because people aren't paying attention as closely as you are. They have their own issues, goals, and dilemmas to preoccupy them. As advertisers on TV understand, you have to repeat your message over and over to get through.

Stakeholders—Who/What/How

When people begin to think about getting help from others, three questions arise: Who should I enlist? What do I want them to do? and How will I go about it? Let's tackle them one at a time.

Who Should You Enlist? The answer will become clear over the next several paragraphs, but we'll start with a quick list of viable candidates as well as the qualifications that might apply to your journey together.

On top of your list might be a good friend at work. Who would you select who doesn't try to compete with you, who doesn't have his or her own agenda in reference to your success, who has *your* best interest at heart?

In listing possible candidates, keep in mind that they can be peers, direct reports, longtime clients, or even competitors you respect. One of the few requirements is that they have the right amount of experience with you. Too much and their cognitive dissonance might get in the way. Too little and they don't have enough data on you to contribute effectively.

On top of the list of qualifications would be their ability, in your estimation, to let go of the past, tell you the truth, and be supportive of you (positive, not negative). There is a last qualification that is far more important than you might realize: their ability to pick something in themselves to improve (this gets them focused more on improvement than on judgment).

Another way of thinking about who you will enlist is in terms of the three foundational roles they can play for you:

- **Thinking partner.** Your thinking partner is someone who can consider you from the *outside looking in*. It's always easy to see patterns in others that we might be blind to in ourselves. The eye-opener for most parents as their kids grow up occurs when they begin to see themselves in their children (not always their good habits, either). It is far easier to see out than in, and it's their job to provide suggestions as well as observations.

- **Live support line.** Unlike a computer manufacturer's live tech support function, which is usually long on tech and short on support, your live support line is a role that is perhaps light on tech but heavy on support. You need a fresh point of view that wants you to succeed and will stay on the line as long as it takes.

- **Accountability insurance.** Your accountability insurance is a stakeholder whose role is to keep you on track, keep your conversations focused, and help you avoid the left-field trips we all end up on if we're not careful.

Some final thoughts on who you might want to enlist lie within another triad:

- It shouldn't be a chore for them to get in touch with you.
- They should already be taking a genuine interest in your life.
- There must be no judging (by you).

Inviting this individual or these individuals into your journey moves it from a cerebral activity (one that goes on only in your mind) into the behavioral realm—something someone else can see. By adding them into the mix, you inject additional motivation (*you* don't want to disappoint *them*) and additional commitment (*they* want to see *you* succeed).

What Do You Want Them to Do? Our mantra in helping successful people change is self-selected change (you pick what to change, no one else) and self-selected raters. By this we mean that once you pick what you want to improve, you also select who you want to go to for three very important ingredients:

- **Feedback on current performance.** How you're doing now on stopping what you've selected to stop.
- **Feed*Forward* on ideas for the future.** Providing suggestions for what you might want to try in giving up ineffective habits (there are very specific directions on this most important step later in this chapter).
- **Peer coaching on a regular basis.** To help you keep track of growth and slippage.

These three ingredients are what you will be asking for from your stake-holders. By common definition, a stakeholder is just about anyone who has an interest in a matter, anyone who stands to gain or lose. In practice, the term can mean just the opposite. In one case, it can be someone with no "skin" in the matter who acts as a neutral party to "hold the stakes" (as in a bet between two parties). In this case, the stakeholder is holding the stakes in a bet between you and yourself. He or she has nothing to gain other than see you win.

How Will You Go about Involving Others? In your efforts to better empathize and eliminate ineffective habits, "how" is relatively simple (but remember the simple-is-not-easy axiom):

> **Once you have selected them, tell them as succinctly as possible about your goals and the bad habit you hope to eliminate.**

Ask them if you may come to them for one or all of the three key ingredients (feedback, Feed*Forward,* and peer coaching).

For the simple feedback component, ask them if you may come to them monthly (biweekly if once a month is insufficient) for their observations of your behavior in reference to what you'd like to stop.

Finally, let them know what to expect of you in receiving the feedback: active listening; no interruptions; allowing them to complete their own sentences; no judgment, explanation, justification, or rationalization; and a simple thank you for their input.

Let this soak in for a few minutes—put the book down. You know what you want to give up; you have criteria for stakeholder roles, selec-

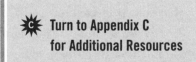

**Turn to Appendix C
for Additional Resources**

tion, and expectations. Go now to Appendix C. Take a moment to write down the names of some candidates for the individuals who will hold the stakes in your personal efforts to be more effective. Go with your gut on *who* to enlist; we can provide advice about *how* they can help you.

GETTING IDEAS: PRACTICING FEED*FORWARD*

We finished the last section with some very simple instructions on how to ask for and receive feedback. Feedback most likely would be acknowledged by everyone as an integral component of growth and change. As we go about the business of becoming, we first need to know something about the past—we need to know where *here* is before we can get there. By selecting the right stakeholders and soliciting their feedback, you can craft and maintain a steady, rolling picture of where you are now.

But there is a problem or limitation with feedback: It focuses on something that has already taken place. Any time you ask about how you're doing, the information you receive is about the past, about what you've done previously. When it comes to behavior, we propose that it's not that It doesn't matter what you do; it's just that it only matters what you do *now*.

The Feed*Forward* Process

Over many years we've collectively led thousands of participants through an exciting exercise called Feed*Forward*. By definition, Feed*Forward* is what to do now, and it's a process that you can learn right here, right now.

In this exercise participants are asked to take on two parallel roles. In the first role you are asked to provide Feed*Forward*—to give others suggestions for the future when asked. In the second role you are asked to solicit and receive suggestions for the future. The activity usually lasts about 15 minutes, with most participants taking part in six or seven mini-dialogues. During the process, participants are asked to do the following:

- **Pick a behavior** that they would like to change (you've already done that).
- **Pair up** with another individual and succinctly describe the behavior to their partner of the moment (e.g., "I'd like to stop using tension as

a tool in my interactions with clients; I don't want them to feel pressured into buying").

- **Ask for Feed*Forward*:** two suggestions that might effect a positive change in the selected behavior.
- **Listen actively** to suggestions and write down a note in reference to each suggestion. No comments are allowed while "listening"; it's what we call the seven seconds of silence.
- **Thank the other participant** for his or her suggestions.
- **Ask the other person** what he or she would like to change.
- **Provide Feed*Forward* to the other person** in the form of two suggestions targeted at helping that person make the positive behavioral change he or she has outlined.
- **Say "You're welcome"** when thanked for your suggestions. The entire process of giving and receiving Feed*Forward* should take two to three minutes at most.
- **Find another partner** and keep repeating the exercise until told to stop.

That's it: giving and receiving suggestions, listening, saying thank you, and trying to get as many suggestions as possible in a very short period.

You can use this technique with as many people as you like, and it doesn't have to take place in a classroom or workshop atmosphere. Don't feel that you can involve only people who know you solely through business. You can get great creative ideas from friends, relatives, neighbors, and even the person you've just met sitting next to you on the plane.

Try it. Keep the "good ideas" and disregard the rest without having to discuss them, defend them, or digress into the same old organizational pity party that seems to doom any productive conversation. In a seminar setting most will gain up to 15 quick suggestions, and at the end of the exercise we ask all the participants to look over their lists of suggestions received and answer the following questions:

> Did you receive a suggestion you would not have come up with on
>   your own?

Does the suggestion seem interesting enough that you think you
  might try it?

The usual affirmative response is greater than 85 percent. In a very short
period, usually in a room full of strangers, almost all practitioners of Feed*Forward* receive multiple suggestions that they consider valuable to them personally. We ask people to provide one word that describes their reaction to or
description of the exercise. We ask them to complete the following sentence:
"This Feed*Forward* exercise was . . ." The responses we usually get are: "great,"
"fun," "easy," "helpful," "useful," and "valuable."

When was the last time you heard a feed*back* process described as fun?
There are myriad reasons why Feed*Forward* works, and we believe you'll find
that there are lots of good reasons to give it a try:

- **We can change the future.** Sorry, the past is gone. It may be useful
  for keeping score, but the future is the only place where we can be someone else.
- **Feed*Forward* is well suited to the needs of successful people.** You
  appreciate ideas aimed at helping you achieve your goals because you
  make the ultimate decision on implementation, no one else.
- **Feed*Forward* can come from anyone.** You don't need to know me, lead
  me, or live with me to provide good counsel.
- **We don't take it personally.** Theoretically, even feedback is supposed to
  be about performance, not personality. But in practice, we take feedback
  personally. It's natural law. Feed*Forward,* however, is not about who we
  are; it's about who we *might be.*
- **Feed*Forward* is efficient,** feeding the needs of successful, driven people.
  Feedback almost inevitably degenerates into a significant time commitment for both parties involved.
- **We listen better to Feed*Forward* than to feedback.** By requiring seven
  seconds of silence and prohibiting any response other than "thank you,"
  we don't engage in the evaluative listening practices of only pretending
  to pay enough attention to craft a reply (sound familiar?).

Understand that there is safety in Feed*Forward* for both the giver and the receiver. For you when you ask for suggestions, there is the knowledge that the other person will not be bringing up your personal history of failures, embarrassments, or missed opportunities. For those of us who like to talk, we have had countless people tell us that the emphasis on silence broken only by "thank you" helps them listen, in some cases for the first time in their lives.

One person explained, "I don't know why, but I always feel like I'm supposed to say something profound or interesting when I'm talking with people. Using this process, knowing that I cannot interrupt and can only say 'thank you' enabled me to focus more on what the person was saying as opposed to thinking about how I was going to respond. It helped me listen."

For the giver of information there is safety too. When asked for their opinion, most people are flattered. They like the idea that someone is interested in getting advice from them. What people don't like is being judged, and if we aren't careful, saying anything other than "thank you" can come across as judging.

Let's assume that someone asks you for a couple of suggestions. To the first suggestion you reply, "Thank you so much; that's a great idea." To the second suggestion you respond, "Good, thanks." To the third suggestion you smile, nod, and say "Uh huh, thanks." No problem, right? You thanked them each time—but what message came across? "Great" . . . "Good" . . . "Uh huh." Even without trying, a hierarchy of judgment was rendered. How interested will they be offering suggestions next time? Remember, *you're thanking them not for the content of their ideas but for willingly helping you.* Silence, a smile, and a "thank you" keep the entire process positive and future-focused.

You've gotten help, and now that you own a process for mining the good thinking of those you value and trust, you've gotten ideas. Now, let's get *there* through a powerful follow-up technique that turns good intentions into behavioral change.

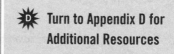
Turn to Appendix D for Additional Resources

GETTING THERE: FOLLOWING UP VIA PEER COACHING

Imagine any one of the following scenarios. They have all happened at some point, and they happen all the time. How about in your organization?

Scenario 1. We leave a sales meeting or training program with a commitment to change, with inspired ideas on how to develop and grow. But for some reason, nothing happens. As Stephen Covey would point out, the urgent gets in the way of the important, and the excitement and commitment fade to black.

Scenario 2. These authors were sitting in the boardroom of a Fortune 100 company with the executive vice president, who posed a perfectly reasonable question: "Does anyone who goes through these development programs ever really change?" At the time, we didn't know.

Scenario 3. Organizational managers from sales and line units as well as the learning and development functions are challenging our industry to provide more than just an event. In the same breath, we are forced to limit our contact with their staff to six to eight contact hours.

The sales arena isn't the only one operating under new management. Performance improvement also has undergone an enormous transformation in accountability for impact and a demonstrable connection to business results and return on expectations, if not on investment. We have learned a great deal in the process.

We now know that although virtually 100 percent of those who take part in our personal development efforts say that they intend to go back and apply what they've learned on the job, somewhat less than 70 percent actually do anything differently in the eyes of their stakeholders. This we know from a database of over 86,000 participants across the spectrum of global organizations, and we see it as a reflection of human nature.

We also know from our research with sales organizations specifically that there is a statistically verifiable link between sales training and behavioral coaching efforts and improvements in day-to-day business measures of revenue and gross profit. These improvements ran anywhere from a 5-point swing to revenue increases of over 26 percent (at a better gross profit too.).

What makes the difference? What's the difference between the 70 percent who at least effect some change and the 30 percent who don't? The difference between those who show small improvements and those who post spectacular gains?

Follow-Up

If we have learned nothing else from our collective findings over these combined 100 years, we have learned three important lessons:

- **Not everyone responds to behavioral development efforts.** For all the reasons we've already covered, we have come to realize that it depends not on us but on *you*, on your desire and commitment to change. You make it work or not.
- **There is a difference between understanding and doing.** Countless development efforts revolve around one huge but false assumption: If people understand, they will do. There is a visceral, tangible difference: One is a cerebral exercise, the other an exercise in the physical world.
- **People don't get better without follow-up.** Becoming a better salesperson is a process, not an event. The process is eerily like that of physical exercise. How many of us have purchased and read an exercise book? How many still have the book, perhaps on the catchall family room bookshelf, and still carry the extra weight we were so motivated to get rid of? There is a significant difference between understanding and doing—that difference is follow-up.

During research across 11,000 people and 86,000 participating responders, it was found that those perceived as having done no follow-up were no more effective than they were at the start. Here's the powerful data: Those who were perceived by their stakeholders as having frequently or consistently followed up with those stakeholders jumped dramatically in their effectiveness.

Let's take a case study specifically from the sales realm. From our research with a leading North American distributor of industrial products and services, we worked within a 2,700-member inside sales team. Some were in a control group that received no intervention, some took part in one of our sales training programs, and other groups participated voluntarily at different levels in our follow-up coaching process.

For context, the control group's sales went down 3.7 percent comparing six months after the events to six months prior. The sales and service reps who participated only in the one-day sales training program saw their revenue increase 1.1 percent when comparing the six months after the training to the six months prior (a great result in itself).

Are you ready for the success story? Those who participated in the training and then engaged in an average of just eight 30-minute phone and e-mail exchanges—just four hours total of follow-up—saw their sales results skyrocket 19.8 percent. As was mentioned a little earlier, these reps saw the increases in revenue take place not at the 20 percent gross margin of the control group but at 29 percent.

What do we conclude?

There is a demonstrable, statistically valid connection between our development practices, especially the follow-up factor, and the business end-result variables of sales and profit.

We can change the paradigm of personal development as an event through follow-up coaching (and we have good reason to do so).

We have heard it said that "follow-up coaching is not training, but it is the missing element in most training that makes it effective."

As Peter Drucker put it in *The Daily Drucker*, "It is not whether the answer is right or wrong but whether it works." This process *works*.

What to Do: Peer Coaching

You get back to your territory, and the phone starts ringing with customer requests, the e-mails need a response, and there is paperwork that must be submitted by tomorrow. The "won't take long but must be done" activities that happen daily start to crowd out the important things. Does it really matter if you delay your development activity for a day to process an urgent customer need? Of course not. How about delaying a week? Not so bad either. But of course what happens is that without follow-up we never get started or we start but never gain momentum.

Building a support system sounds good, but for a lot of salespeople it is not easy. Sales *is* different from just about every other job in the organization. In many, if not most, organizations, each salesperson has his or her sales results posted for all to see on a monthly, weekly, or even daily basis. Unlike most of the people in the organization, competition between salespeople is encouraged.

Others go to the office daily, sit within several feet of their peers, and have meetings with team members or lunch with colleagues every day. In the natural course of doing business they develop relationships with people at work. Sales *is* different. Salespeople are often alone. Lunch usually is eaten by oneself. It can be lonely, and no one was volunteering to provide live, professional behavioral coaching the last time you checked your e-mail.

If you could implement a process that costs virtually nothing, takes about 10 minutes a day, can be done from anywhere at any time of day, and—if you stick with it—will help you achieve positive, measurable behavioral change, would you give it a try? It is a tool called peer coaching. Like Feed*Forward,* peer coaching is made to order for the hectic life rhythms of salespeople. It is a "Daily Questions" process. Here is how it has worked in our lives.

Marshall. Marshall has a peer coach named Jim. Just about every night, regardless of where either of them is in the world, it's Jim's job as his coach to call Marshall and ask him questions. For Marshall the questions are mostly about physical well-being and fitness habits as he spends some 200 days a year on planes, trains, and automobiles (and hotel rooms). Marshall wrote the questions, and it is Jim's job to ask the questions of Marshall.

They are the same questions every night and revolve around topics such as "On a scale of 1 to 10, how happy are you today?" "How much walking did you do today?" "How many push-ups, how many sit-ups?" That's it. Seventeen questions in all—17 questions of importance to Marshall that relate to the changes he wants to effect in his life. All the questions must be those that can be answered only by yes, no, a name, or a number. This keeps the calls short and to the point. The nightly call is an enforced follow-up process, and though the questions evolve over time, Marshall and Jim manage to make the calls about 80 percent of the time. If they miss a night, they make it up next time. Jim has a set of questions that Marshall asks of him on each call as well—both are coach *and* coachee.

Don. Don has a peer coach named Brant, a 20-year friend from his days in San Diego. Their calls have been scheduled for the same time every Monday and Thursday—twice a week, 1:00 p.m. Pacific Time/4:00 p.m. Eastern Time. In Don's case, the questions have been structured a little differently than Marshall's. Three general *values* areas grounded the questions he wanted Brant to ask: "well-being," which includes nutrition and fitness questions; "relationships," which includes questions about his efforts with family, friends, and professional associates; and "purpose," which includes questions around his efforts in service to others and his own personal growth.

As with Marshall, Don's questions evolved over time, and Don also asks Brant a set of questions generated by Brant during each call. Don and Brant have taken breaks in the questioning process at times but come back to it as something that works for them.

The Daily Questions Process

Daily Questions is regular, structured, efficient follow-up to behavioral goal setting. Here are the steps you should follow to make it work:

Step 1: Designing Questions. The first step in implementing a Daily Questions program is to design questions that will focus you on the exact behaviors you want to affect. The key is that you write your own questions. They must be able to be answered with either yes, no, or with a name or number. Start with the ineffective habit you selected earlier in the book. What behaviors do you want to decrease to make that change happen, and what might you want to do more of?

Consider the important issues in your life that you want to improve on and think of some small daily behaviors that would affect each issue. One tip: Think small. Select several small changes rather than a major change that might overwhelm your day. Do you want to make more effective sales calls, stop curb qualifying, or follow up more effectively? Design questions like the following:

- How many sales calls did I make today?
- How many times did I interrupt someone today?
- Did I allow seven seconds of silence to listen to someone today?

This process works so well that we have expanded it beyond professional questions to questions that will help you improve other important facets of your life. In Appendix E we've included a sample chart to get you started with your own questions.

There is no magic number of questions to list. Some people select only a few questions targeted at a specific area of their lives, such as improving their current effectiveness on the job. Others pick questions that affect both their personal and professional lives. The most we have heard of is 25, and the least is 3. The key is that they are your questions. They have meaning to *you*.

Step 2: Selecting a Peer Coach. Now that you have your questions, you need to select a peer coach who is a buddy. By that we mean someone who is interested in your life and has your best interests in mind. It can be almost anyone. It can be a friend, neighbor, family member, or peer. The key is that this person cares. The good news is that you are going to ask for only a few minutes of her time each day. But it is going to be *every day* or two to three times per week.

The person needs to have some motivation to become involved. What will help him buy in is that this can work for him as well. Have this person develop some questions that you will ask him each day so that the process is reciprocal.

With that in mind, a fellow salesperson in your organization is an ideal peer coach. Even in the most competitive sales forces, friendships evolve. Pick a peer coach and help each other build your individual effectiveness. This is like selecting stakeholders: It shouldn't be a chore for them or for you, you should be interested in each other's lives, and both of you should be free of judgment.

Step 3: Scheduling. The third step is to schedule your phone calls. In today's cell phone world your location and access to a telephone are not an issue. In fact, a lot of people consciously schedule times (remember, it is only a few minutes) when they know they will be in the car, at an airport, or in a hotel room. The key is to schedule them for a specific time and identify who will be calling whom. We have found that scheduling usually works and "we'll call each other tomorrow sometime" does not.

Step 4: Making the Calls. You might think that asking someone to call you every day without your paying her is asking a lot, but remember that there is something in it for both of you. The key in this step is that the coach can ask only the prescribed questions, write down the answers, and provide only positive feedback (if appropriate). *No negative feedback.* No matter what the other person has done, the coach says nothing that might produce guilt. The coach cannot judge your answers, ask additional questions, or provide additional observations or feedback other than supportive gestures that reinforce success.

Step 5: Recording Data. In the fifth step you use an Excel spreadsheet or something similar to send the results to each other on a monthly basis. There is no need to include commentary; just send the yes/no or numeric data to your peer coach.

Some people say, "Couldn't you accomplish the same thing by writing all this information in a diary or just generate a computer list that you fill out daily instead of involving a friend?" Although that might work, it doesn't have the same likelihood of success. The key to peer coaching is that it involves another person besides you. How many of us have started a diary but got busy, got out of the habit, and eventually stopped writing in it? The key to a buddy coach is that we don't want to disappoint him or her (that is human nature). Even if we are tired or busy or distracted, if we said we were going to call at 7:00 p.m., we are likely to do it.

Peer coaching works for several reasons:

1. **In a very time-efficient manner, peer coaching holds you accountable for results.** Knowing that someone you like and respect will be calling tonight and asking, "Did you openly apologize to a customer today?" will keep you focused. Even though you know there will be no judgment or negatives, you don't want to let your coach down.

2. **The process provides support for success.** That same person you like and respect gives you immediate positive recognition. You start feeling better about the progress you're making toward success.

3. **You are able to see measurable results in the monthly spreadsheets.** So many times change is hard to quantify. Are you really more effective now than you were three months ago? The spreadsheets document progress in specific areas. You can see measurable results.

Just as with any change initiative, you are not going to see immediate results. But if you stick with it for a few months, make the daily calls, and answer the questions, the results will appear. Give it the same 90 days you would any sales promotion. You will feel better, and people will notice.

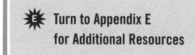

Turn to Appendix E for Additional Resources

What does follow-up—specifically, follow-up through peer coaching—embody? It is how we measure our progress and how we remind others (as well as ourselves) that we're making an effort to change. It is how we mentally imprint our change efforts by embodying a built-in acknowledgment of positive movement or progress toward those efforts. It is also a mechanism for banishing skepticism in ourselves and others, but mostly it is focused, purposeful action toward self-improvement. Make it part of your life.

So What? What did you learn?

■ Changing perception. It takes two people to change: one to change and another to notice.

■ The who, what, and how of enlisting stakeholders in your change efforts

■ Practicing Feed*Forward*—working toward a better future

■ With follow-up we get better; with peer coaching we can document it.

Now What? What might you do now?

■ Contact your stakeholders. Invite them to help you and to pick something to change in themselves.

■ Set up regular brief encounters with your stakeholders to solicit Feed*Forward* suggestions.

■ Call your peer coach candidate right now to talk about the process. It works.

Are We There Yet?

A final summary of our thoughts on the new game of customer influence and a farewell wish for you—happy sales!

- Take in the rules of the new game of selling.
- Discover what thousands of successful people have taught us about their personal change efforts.
- Understand what might get in the way of change and learn how to avoid the traps.
- Gain perspective on what matters most and when it matters most in the workplace and at home.
- Personally envision a means to happiness now, not when.

A Look to the Future: Be Present to Ask, Learn, Follow Up, and Grow   12

If you've ever purchased a raffle ticket for a school fund-raiser or entered a contest of chance, you have seen the tag disclaimer "Need not be present to win." The first rule of selling in the new millennium requires just the opposite: You *must* be present to win. To be effective in sales, we know we have to possess the capacity to be comfortably present in front of anyone, with our attention in the present time, and be able to do that on purpose. In Chapter 3 we explored the critical nature of the state of the moment with another person: the ability to be present and even to confront. This doesn't mean having a confrontation; it means being able to be *with* a person without flinching or avoidance—being fully aware of that person and paying attention to her with comfort.

This is a new game. Selling is different, buying is different, and the rules are different. "Must be present in order to win" is the first rule of the new game, but what else will it take? In a nutshell—ask, learn, follow up, and grow. It is not a telling world anymore—no one person can be smart enough—but effectiveness is available for the asking.

ASK

The effective seller of the future consistently will ask a variety of key stakeholders for ideas, opinions, and feedback. Vital sources of information will include present and potential customers, suppliers, team members, cross-divisional peers, direct reports, managers, other members of the organization, researchers, and thought leaders. The sales leader will ask in a variety of ways: through inventories, satisfaction surveys, phone calls, voice mail, e-mail, the Internet, satellite, and *in person.*

The trend toward asking is already very clear. Twenty years ago too few top sellers ever asked for feedback. Today the majority of the most highly respected sales leaders in every industry regularly ask for feedback. As you've seen, they do so in companies such as Nike, Abbott, SYKES, and Ford, and the trend is growing rapidly around the world.

Aside from the obvious benefit of gaining new ideas and insights, the habit of asking by top sellers has a secondary benefit that may be just as important. A salesperson who asks is providing a role model for others. Sincere asking demonstrates a willingness to learn, a desire to serve, and a humility that can be an inspiration for the entire organization.

LEARN

Peter Senge has written extensively about the future importance of the learning organization. A learning organization will need to be populated with people who model continuous learning in their day-to-day behavior. Two keys to learning are (1) effective listening and (2) reflection after asking for and receiving information. Asking for input and then shooting the messenger who delivers the bad news is worse than not asking at all.

A major challenge for the learner of the future will be prioritization. We all face the danger of drowning in the sea of information we've talked about. There is more to learn than any human can process: Some 200,000 texts are sent every second, and 107 trillion e-mails hit our collective in-box last year. Top sellers will need to learn the vital areas for change from each source of information they select. Although you need to receive input more frequently and from more sources, the time available to process this information will be declining. We will exist in a world that is characterized by downsizing and ongoing reengineering. We need to get more work done, get it done faster, and get it done with considerably less support staff.

In the private sector, there are no indications that global competition will decrease in the future or that sellers will have more time and more staff. In the social sector, there are no indications that human needs will decrease or that the government will take care of more social problems. Sales professionals who can ask, process information, and learn in a highly efficient manner will have a tremendous competitive advantage over their slower and less proactive competitors.

FOLLOW-UP

When measuring the success of efforts toward personal behavioral change in leaders or salespeople, very few organizations measure anything other than reactions to the process, in other words, whether the participants liked what they went through. Something like 80 percent measure only this reaction to the process, and over a 40-year span only 7 percent actually assessed the impact of building positive, measurable behavioral change against the bottom-line metrics of revenue and profit. We have done so with our clients, and with conviction (and data) we can say: "With follow-up you get better."

We happen to believe that training docs in fact equip today's workforce to compete more effectively, yet our position has always been that a training event alone is only a beginning, a launch. Many clients decry the flavor of the month nature of human skills development yet ask what can be done in six hours or less. This was not the case with one client we've already mentioned who was eager to break the event paradigm and document just how much of a difference we could make.

Our client was a leading North American distributor of industrial products and services. Bearings, belts, fasteners, and fluids are just a few of the tens of thousands of parts they represented. Customers of the client ran the gamut from smaller job shops and walk-in customers to the largest national accounts, from automotive to food processing and durable goods. With our study, inside salespeople made up the participant pool (the organization has approximately 3,000 total).

Participants in our research were organized into four basic groups: the *control* group, which received no intervention; the *trained* group, which received one day of our sales development; the *volunteered* group, which received one day of training and then volunteered for follow-up telecoaching; and the *coached* group, which received one day of training, volunteered for the follow-up, and then stayed with the follow-up for an average of eight 30-minute telecoaching conversations. Sales and gross profit data for the six months before and after the training dates were compared to see if those who participated sold more than those who did not.

With statistical validity and reliability, each level of increased involvement and follow-up correlated with increased sales and gross profit. Simply put, those who did nothing saw their sales drop almost 4 percent, those who participated in eight hours of training saw their sales rise by 1 percent, and those who volunteered and stayed with the follow-up saw their sales increase between 9 and 19 percent. Those who stayed with the follow-up coaching returned 20 times the growth of those who only attended an event.

Follow-up will be a key challenge for the seller of the future. Asking and learning will have to be more than an academic exercise. The process will have to produce meaningful, positive change. By learning how to follow up efficiently and effectively in an extremely busy world, sellers of the future will enable their key stakeholders to see the positive actions that result. With follow-up, we get better—period.

GROW

The seller of the future will have to change and grow on the job. Can this happen? Definitely yes. Those who reach out, ask for input, learn, respond in a positive manner, involve key stakeholders, and follow up almost invariably will be seen as becoming more effective and growing over time. As demands increase, effective personal growth and development will become more important than ever. However, the methodology of personal development may change radically.

Historically, development efforts have tended to focus on the "front side" of the development process: impressive training, well-designed forms, clever slogans, and lots of flash. They have not focused on the "back side" of the process: the ongoing application of what is being learned. Follow-up studies have validated the obvious: What we do back on the job is more meaningful than what we do in the classroom.

Future selling skills development will not be like getting in shape; it will be like *staying* in shape. The program of the month has the same impact as the crash-diet approach to physical fitness: The results don't last. In the future, far more emphasis will be placed on developing the processes required to ensure positive, ongoing personal growth. By developing and working processes that ensure ongoing asking, learning, and following up, you *can* be present for your customers, you *can* maintain the empathy that connects you to them, and you *can* increase your sales in an increasingly volatile environment.

Don't Give Up: Final Thoughts on Change

An old Latin proverb can be paraphrased to read "The wise learn from the mistakes of others." In our collective 100 years of professional experience we've made many mistakes. We've seen the interpersonal debris in the wake of many mistakes, our own as well as those of others. Over the years—separate and apart from this book—we've personally taken to keeping a "This I Know" book of sayings, quotes, and truisms as a gift to our children. We don't know exactly where the idea came from; it might have been Oprah, or it might have been something we read. Regardless of its origins, it's meaningful, personal, and, we hope, helpful.

In this chapter of final thoughts we would like to increase the odds that you will profit from our mistakes and from what we've learned as well as what we have come to know in our journey of applying these concepts of change to the profession of sales. Here is what we have come to know.

HI-TECH/NO-TOUCH DOESN'T WORK

The hi-tech/no-touch approach to customer contact blindly embraced by far too many organizations is a recipe for disaster. Customers may prefer a particular product or brand, but they are loyal to *people*. The disingenuous positioning of a no-touch interface as a customer convenience—rather than acknowledging the cost-containment strategy that in fact drives it—will come back to haunt us.

FUNCTIONAL FIRST

Mastery of the functional arena will allow you to enter the game. Effectiveness in the human arena will allow you to compete—and win.

CHOOSE EMPATHY

Choosing empathy over victory will counter the traditionally ingrained paradigm of us versus them in customer interactions. These are the habits our customers want us to take up. Choose to focus on the organic connection possible between all of us. Balance ego with empathy; choose rapport. The more you subordinate your need to shine, the more you shine in people's eyes—what a paradox.

MAKE ROOM FOR POSITIVE BEHAVIORS

We once were given an awesome suggestion by a workshop participant in reference to our closets at home. The suggestion was that whenever you buy new clothes, make room for them by giving up something else in there. If you buy new pants, find a pair to donate. If you purchase a half dozen pairs of socks, find six in a drawer for the Goodwill bag. In choosing an ineffective behavioral habit to give up, what you often do is make room for more effective behaviors with your customers. Learn to enjoy the shift into neutral and give something up.

EMBRACE "WHAT GOT YOU HERE . . . WILL NOT GET YOU THERE"

It is no longer possible to ride out a career on a single set of behaviors. Right now, the average length of time someone stays in a job is 4.1 years and dropping. Mix in college, relationships, children, illness—and 8 to 14 job or career changes over a lifetime—and you'll find that your natural state will be one of change. Your life will not be static.

BEFORE YOU TREAT, DOUBLE-CHECK YOUR DIAGNOSIS

Make sure that you have a disease that behavioral change can cure. We watch many industries start their day with a morning sales rally that includes a review of the products or services they want to move and a rousing reiteration of the incentives for the salesperson to move a featured product *today.*

Would it be a surprise if the salesperson then charged out to propagandize or use tension as a tool to make the sale? When sales managers insist—no, *demand*—that their people call on a particular-size prospect each and every week (sometimes even when the salesperson has been asked by the prospect not to call), is it any wonder that the salesperson makes a habit of contact without purpose?

Under certain business models you may have to choose between organizationally mandated practices and what you intuitively know to be the right practice. Only you can make the call.

NARROW IT DOWN

Don't try to do it all. This is another of the success traps to avoid. We often have to work very hard at convincing successful people that not everything needs fixing. Would you say, being as busy as you are, that perhaps the root cause lies within your tendency to never say no? The old adage "The reward for a job well done is more work" most likely was written about you. Let this be one part of your life where you don't over commit—pick *one* thing to stop doing.

KNOW YOUR ENEMIES

When it comes to positive, measurable, lasting behavioral change, the deck is often stacked against you.

Time

"I had no idea that this process would take so long. I'm not sure it's worth it."

Habits neither appear nor disappear overnight. Goal setters have a chronic tendency to underestimate the time needed to reach targets. In setting goals for behavioral change, it's important to be realistic about the time needed to produce positive, lasting results. Habits that have taken years to develop won't go away in a week. Set time expectations that are 50 to 100 percent longer than you think you will need to see results and then add a little more.

Effort

"This is a lot harder than I thought it would be. It sounded so simple when we were starting out."

Like any exercise, it takes discipline. The optimism bias of goal setters applies to difficulty and effort as well as time. Not only does everything take longer than we think it will, it requires more hard work than we anticipate.

In setting goals, it is important to accept the fact that real change requires real work. Acknowledging the price for success at the beginning of the change process will help prevent the disappointment that can occur when challenges arise later (and they will).

Distractions

"I would really like to work toward my goal, but I'm facing some unique challenges right now. It might be better if I just stopped and did this at a time when things weren't so crazy."

We are as busy as we have ever been. Goal setters have a tendency to underestimate the distractions and competing goals that invariably appear throughout the year. Here is a piece of advice we give coaching clients: "We're not sure what crisis will appear, but we're almost positive that some crisis will appear."

Plan for distractions in advance. Assume that crazy is the new normal; you will be closer to the reality that awaits you.

Rewards and Ownership

"I wasn't sure that this would work in the first place. I tried it out, and it didn't do that much good. As I guessed, this was kind of a waste of time."

After we see some improvement, we don't get the praise we expected from others. The mistakes of thinking that something will make us better and that others are laser-focused on what we are doing both belong in the arena of ownership. After years of experience in helping real people change real behavior in the real world, we've learned a hard lesson: Only you will make you better. When it comes down to it, only you are watching. To have a real chance for success, you have to take personal ownership and have the internal belief that this will work if, and only if, I make it work, and I will make it work—for me.

Maintenance

"I think I did actually try to change and get better, but I have let it slide since then. What am I supposed to do, work on this for the rest of my life?"

Once we hit our goal, we forget how hard it is to stay in shape. Once the goal setter has put in all the effort needed to achieve a goal, it can be tough for her to face the reality of what's needed to maintain the new status quo. Only 17 percent of smokers who quit do so without backsliding. Only 5 percent of dieters reach their target weight, and only 0.5 percent maintain it.

Here are the cold, hard truths. Real change requires real effort. The quick fix is seldom a meaningful one. Distractions and things that compete for your attention are going to come up frequently. Changing any type of behavior won't solve all of life's problems, and any meaningful change probably will require a lifetime of effort.

THERE IS NO IDEAL BEHAVIOR

Understand and accept that there's always someone who is taller/shorter, faster/slower, richer/poorer, or better/worse than you. This is all about you, not you in comparison to someone else. Pick one issue that matters to you and attack it until it doesn't matter anymore.

KEEP SCORE

If you can measure it, you can change it. We ask you in the process of peer coaching to craft questions that can be answered only with yes, no, a name, or a number. You can track those answers; the parameters never vary. Don't worry about some endgame; we applaud our clients when they begin the process of fixing their flaws, not just at the end.

YOU GO FIRST

The time is *now*. How much of our limited lifetimes do we spend, both on the job and at home, bemoaning the awful, ineffective, unproductive, and downright mean-spirited habits of others? We do it in our cars, as we watch news on TV, as we surf the Web. We complain about how so many need to mend their ways and make this a better planet. Our advice is: *You* go first. Save your energy. Ask yourself, What am *I* willing to change right now? Just do that—it's more than enough.

Happy Sales   CODA

Sales is, as we've said, *different:* different from other professions, different from other aspirations, different from other lives.

Inherent in the realm of customer contact is the focus on organizational data and with that the quantification (through the coin of the realm) of all that we do in the short term and the long. Inherent in sales are both external and artificial measures of what matters; this is all a given.

However, across not just sales but almost any organizational function you can dream up, there are *organizational* metrics and there are *personal* metrics. We work with our participants on what really matters to *them.* In fact, we tell them that on their deathbeds, when they look around the room, they probably will not see anyone from their current employer. We ask our customers to take a deep breath and imagine themselves at age 95, given the gift of being able to counsel themselves at their current age. We ask, "What would you tell the current you? What advice does the old you have for today's you in both your professional life and your personal life?" We have asked these questions countless times, and the answers are now predictable.

We also have reviewed research on aging to find out what matters to those nearing the end of their lives as well as research on happiness among the highly successful who outwardly already have everything they need. Can you guess the patterns we discovered?

As a hint, here's a quote from Samuel Clemens, aka Mark Twain: "I am an old man now. I have seen lots of trouble; most of it never happened."

So much of what we agonize over from our teens to middle age takes place between our ears. From those approaching life's end and from those who have in almost every measure achieved success, the "what matters" on a professional level is meaning, contribution, and happiness. On a personal level, they have discovered that life may not be fair, but it is good.

Overwhelmingly, the advice is to let go of any imagined injustices in your life because the goal is one of completion. Think about it. What do you tend to put off at work or at home? What and *who* do you tend to avoid? Are there people with whom you can't quite get comfortable, in whose presence you feel elevated tension? Is it higher-stakes decision making that creates dissonance? Is it starting or ending a significant chapter in your professional or personal life? Is it owning up to a mistake you've made or just acknowledging certain feelings or insecurities?

Carrying too much *weight* can kill you. Carrying too much *wait* exacts its toll in productivity, peace of mind, personal happiness, and effectiveness. At some point wait and see is simply avoidance, not a strategy. What can you do about it?

- **Write it down.** Articulate in writing what and whom you currently avoid: people, decisions, feelings.
- **Take a first step with someone.** Approach the people involved and verbally acknowledge your avoidance and tension. Be open to letting go of past tensions whether they can do it or not. It's not about who is right; it's about how you react to the relationship.
- **Take a last step with someone.** Don't be afraid to let go of the wait in your life. Stop wishing for a better past and look ahead. Sometimes the *letting go* involves someone else.

Completion will set you free. You'll be surprised how good you feel and how much more effective you can be for those you decide to keep in your life.

The second profound piece of advice from those looking back over a long life filled with success and effectiveness is to hold on to your dreams. Whether it is to learn another language or a musical instrument, to travel, to volunteer, or to reconnect to a lost relationship or hobby, keep the dream intact. How? There are a number of tools available to you to help maintain your focus on what matters most. Here are two:

- **Again, write it down.** There is power in the written word. Record your bucket list of what you want to accomplish and post it.
- **Write a letter,** or several, to reconnect with yourself. You don't even have to send them, but you might want to think about articulating your dreams, gratitude, and even advice. Write one to a family member, a friend or associate, someone important to you who has passed, a younger you, or a cherished mentor. Again, articulation helps make it real.

On every level, we counsel fighting tooth and nail the great Western disease "I'll be happy *when . . .*" Most of us are so busy, over solicited, and overcommitted that the following might sound familiar.

> "I'll start using the treadmill when I get this project finished."
> "I'll learn to play golf/guitar/piano when the kids are a little older."
> "I'll take Mom for a ride in a hot air balloon when I'm not quite so busy."

Our parting words? Be happy *now.* Enjoy sales and the process of positive behavioral change; figure out for yourself what will *get you there.*
Happy sales!

Appendix A

Mindful Attention Awareness Scale (Chapter 3)

Instructions: *Following is a collection of statements about your everyday experience. Using the 1–6 scale below, indicate how frequently or infrequently you currently have each experience. Answer according to what really reflects your experience rather than what you think your experience should be. Treat each item separately from every other item.*

	Almost Always	Very Frequently	Somewhat Frequently	Somewhat Infrequently	Very Infrequently	Almost Never
I could be experiencing some emotion and not be conscious of it until sometime later.	1	2	3	4	5	6
I break or spill things because of carelessness, not paying attention, or thinking of something else.	1	2	3	4	5	6
I find it difficult to stay focused on what's happening in the present.	1	2	3	4	5	6
I tend to walk quickly to get where I'm going without paying attention to what I experience along the way.	1	2	3	4	5	6
I tend not to notice feelings of physical tension or discomfort until they really grab my attention.	1	2	3	4	5	6
I forget a person's name almost as soon as I've been told it for the first time.	1	2	3	4	5	6

	Almost Always	Very Frequently	Somewhat Frequently	Somewhat Infrequently	Very Infrequently	Almost Never
It seems I am "running on automatic," without much awareness of what I'm doing.	1	2	3	4	5	6
I rush through activities without being really attentive to them.	1	2	3	4	5	6
I get so focused on the goal I want to achieve that I lose touch with what I'm doing right now to get there.	1	2	3	4	5	6
I do jobs or tasks automatically, without being aware of what I'm doing.	1	2	3	4	5	6
I find myself listening to someone with one ear and doing something else at the same time.	1	2	3	4	5	6
I drive places on automatic pilot and then wonder why I went there.	1	2	3	4	5	6
I find myself preoccupied with the future or the past.	1	2	3	4	5	6
I find myself doing things without paying attention.	1	2	3	4	5	6
I snack without being aware that I'm eating.	1	2	3	4	5	6

MAAS Scoring: To score the scale, simply compute an average of the 15 items. The higher the score, the more present you are on a regular basis.

Appendix B

Choosing What to Stop (Chapter 9)

Instructions: Pick the habit most closely associated with the behaviors you would like to give up to be more effective. Highlight the habit visually. Use the "Key Content" to confirm your selection and then write down the associated behaviors and how you will know the habit doesn't matter anymore.

Habit 1—Failure to Be Present: repeated and annoying displays of behavior that indicate that we would rather be somewhere else, "some*when*" else, or with someone else.

Habit 2—Vocal Filler: the overuse of unnecessary (and meaningless) verbal qualifiers.

Habit 3—Selling Past the Close: the irresistible urge to verbalize and execute every possible step in the sales process.

Habit 4—Selective Hearing: the absence of active listening in the presence of a customer.

Habit 5—Contact without Purpose: repeated deliberate communication for no valid business reason (other than wanting to sell something).

Habit 6—Curb Qualifying: the tendency to judge a prospect's means and motive superficially from a distance.

Habit 7—Using Tension as a Tool: also known as "sale ends Saturday."

Habit 8—One-Upping: the constant need to top our conversational partner in an effort to show the world just how smart we are.

Habit 9—Overfamiliarity: the use of inappropriately intimate gestures.

Habit 10—Withholding Passion and Energy: the tendency to forget that people decide on the basis of emotion and later justify that decision with logic.

Habit 11—Explaining Failure: behaving under the erroneous belief that simply being able to assign blame, fault, or guilt is enough to satisfy the customer.

Habit 12—Never Having to Say You're Sorry: the personal inability to apologize or accept responsibility for personal or organizational error or injury.

Habit 13—Throwing Others under the Bus: sacrificing a colleague—often anonymous, often vulnerable, and usually innocent—with blame for one's own functional failure.

Habit 14—Propagandizing: overreliance on organizational rhetoric and themes.

Habit 15—Wasting Energy: taking part in organizational blame-storming and pity parties.

Habit 16—Obsessing over the Numbers: achieving revenue, profit, or productivity targets at the expense of metrics of a higher calling.

How to Choose What to Stop

Key Content—Narrow it Down:

The Rule of Three—The ideal structure for pattern recognition (and for remembering). Whether the template for humor, drama, literature, music, or the U.S. Marine Corps and the holy trinity, we remember in threes and we manage in threes.

Information or Emotion—Review each of the 16 habits and you'll find that practitioners of any of them suffer from a serious overload or underload of information or emotion. A good start at this point is to look inward when you have difficulties with interpersonal communication. Do they revolve around the dynamics of information or emotion?

Key Content—Gathering Data

Casual Remarks—Become a first-class noticer of what others say about you and what you say about yourself.

The Mute Button—You also have the ability to tune out the words others are using and focus solely on nonverbal communication. Notice physical movement, positioning, proximity, eye contact, and other indicators of interpersonal ease or discomfort. What part do you play in the silent movie?

Take It Home—Show the list of habits to someone who matters to you at home and ask that person to pick one habit that you are most guilty of and one habit that you are least guilty of.

Key Content—*Choosing a Behavior*

Because Of versus In Spite Of—Make sure you aren't suffering from the success delusion.

The Laws of Energy—Change within any context requires energy. Make sure there is a felt need for change that you possess.

Notes _____

_____

_____

_____

_____

_____

_____

_____

_____

_____

Choosing What to Stop: Activity

Instructions: Pick a behavior that matters to you and attack it until it doesn't matter anymore.

To be more effective with those who matter to me (customers, associates, family, friends), I would like to stop: _____

_____

_____

_____

_____

Related "habit": _____

How I will know that it doesn't matter anymore: _____

_____

_____

_____

_____

_____

_____

_____

_____

_____

Appendix C

Getting Help (Chapter 11)

Instructions: Review the following ideas surrounding the recruitment of your stakeholders. Record the names of the individuals you will go to for help and what role you would like them to play. Then compose a scripting of exactly what you will say to each of them.

- **Dissonance versus harmony.** Human beings view others in a manner that is consistent with our existing stereotypes (positive or negative). You have to improve 100 percent to get 10 percent credit.

- **Advertising.** Your odds of success increase considerably if you tell people that you are trying to change and are very specific about what you want to improve. Now your efforts are on their radar screen.

- **Once isn't enough.** We've known for 100 years that it takes several touches to create awareness, interest, and acceptance in the buying public. Personal change is no different.

- **Stakeholders: who to enlist.** Qualifications include a good friend at work (someone who has your best interest at heart), someone with just the right amount of experience with you and the ability to let go of the past, and someone who will pick something to improve in himself or herself.

- **Stakeholders: what role they play.** Equal parts thinking partner, live support, accountability insurance. What you want from them is feedback: how you're doing currently (Feed*Forward*), ideas for the future and peer coaching—regular two-way involvement.

■ **Stakeholders: how to involve them**. Explain your goals, ask for their help, outline the process, communicate your expectations.

Getting Help Activity: Stakeholder Candidates

Instructions: List five (plus or minus two) stakeholder candidates you believe meet the criteria just discussed. You don't have to go to each one for all three outputs (feedback, Feed Forward, peer coaching). A combination of individuals can provide everything you need.

Candidate/Role: _____

Candidate/Role: _____

Candidate/Role: _____

Candidate/Role: _____

Candidate/Role: _____

Getting Help Activity: Your Request for Help Scripting

Explain my goals—What is the change I am trying to make, and what is the habit I hope to eliminate? _____

_____

_____

_____

Ask for their help—What do I want to come to them for (feedback, Feed*Forward,* peer coaching, or all three)? _____

_____

_____

_____

Outline the process—Meet biweekly, weekly teleconference, face-to-face?

_____

_____

_____

Set expectations—What can they expect of me?
Active listening, no interruptions, judgment, explanations, justification, or
rationalization—and a simple thank you for their input and involvement.

Appendix D

Getting Ideas (Chapter 11): The Feed*Forward* Process

*Instructions: Review the following guidelines for soliciting ideas through Feed*Forward* with a few of your stakeholders. Conduct a short Feed*Forward* session with one to three of them and record the ideas you receive. Get in the habit of asking for suggestions, listening and then simply saying "thank you."*

You are asked to take on two parallel roles. In the first role you are asked to provide Feed*Forward* to give others suggestions for the future when asked. In the second role you are asked to solicit and receive suggestions for the future. The activity will last 15 minutes, with most participants taking part in minidialogues. The process is as follows:

1. **Pair up** with another individual and succinctly describe the behavior you have chosen to stop (for example, "I'd like to stop using tension as a tool in my interactions with clients; I don't want them to feel pressured into buying").
2. **Ask for Feed*Forward*,** from your partner of the moment; ask for two suggestions that might effect a positive change in your selected behavior.
3. **Listen actively** to suggestions and write down a note in reference to each suggestion. No comments are allowed while "listening"; it's what we call the seven seconds of silence.
4. **Thank your partner** for his or her suggestions.
5. **Ask the other person** what he or she would like to change.

6. **Provide Feed*Forward*** to the other person in the form of two suggestions targeted to helping that person make the positive behavioral change he or she has described to you.
7. **Say "You're welcome"** when thanked for your suggestions. The entire process of both giving and receiving Feed*Forward* should take two or three minutes at most.

Selected Behavior: _____

Feed*Forward* Suggestions: _____

_____

_____

_____

_____

_____

_____

_____

_____

_____

_____

_____

_____

_____

_____

_____

_____

_____

Appendix E

Getting There (Chapter 11): Peer Coaching

Getting There Sample Questions Template

Instructions: Develop your list of "Daily Questions" to use with your peer coach. Following is a sample set to start your thinking. Ask your peer coach to write his questions (teach him the process) and schedule your first calls. Don't feel you have to fill in every blank. Pick the questions that matter to you.

Scheduling: Questions must be answered with yes, no, a number, or a name. No negative feedback or discussion. Should be conducted in regular, *scheduled* intervals.

SAMPLE DAILY QUESTIONS

Value	Focus	Questions
Well-Being	Nutrition	• How many "chocolates" today • Did you get a "fruit/veggie" serving in today?
	Fitness	• What do you weigh today? • What was your last run time/distance?
	Spiritual	• Did you pray for patience today? • Are you happy *now*?
Relationships	Family	• Did you deliver a "that looks nice"? • With whom—15 minutes— *TV off?*

(continued)

SAMPLE DAILY QUESTIONS (*continued*)

Value	Focus	Questions
Relationships (*continued*)	Friendship	• With whom did you make a "deposit" today?
	Professional	• **Who did you "contact with purpose" today?** • Did you spend 15 minutes on your "next" career? • Did you "no/but/however" today?
Purpose	Growth	• **Did you read for business development today?** • Did you "write" today?
	Service	• **Who did you help "outside the family"?**
	Transformation	• **Did you use tension as a tool at home today?** • Did you work on the first "set" today?

Questions Template

Daily Instructions: Questions must be answered with yes, no, a number, or a name. No negative feedback or discussion. Calls should be conducted in regular, scheduled intervals.

DAILY QUESTIONS

Value	Focus	Questions
Well-Being	Nutrition	• •
	Fitness	• •
	Spiritual	• •

Relationships	Family	•
		•
		•
	Friendship	•
		•
	Professional	•
		•
		•

Purpose	Growth	•
		•
		•
	Service	•
		•
		•
	Transformation	•
		•
		•

Index

ABOUT THE AUTHORS

Marshall Goldsmith

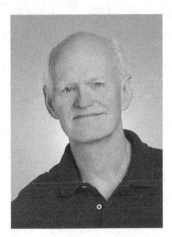

Dr. Marshall Goldsmith is a world authority in helping successful leaders get even better by achieving positive, lasting change in behavior—for themselves, their people, and their teams.

Dr. Goldsmith has been recognized as one of the 15 most influential business thinkers in the world in the biannual study sponsored by *The Times* (London) and *Forbes*. The American Management Association named Marshall as one of 50 great thinkers and leaders who have influenced the field of management over the past 80 years. He is one of only two educators who have won the *Institute of Management Studies* Lifetime Achievement Award. Major business press acknowledgments include *Business Week*—most influential practitioners in the history of leadership development; *Wall Street Journal*—top 10 executive educators; *Forbes*—five most respected executive coaches; *Leadership Excellence*—top five thinkers on leadership; *Economic Times* (India)—top CEO coaches of America; *Economist* (UK)—most credible executive advisors in the new era of business; and *Fast Company*—America's preeminent executive coach.

Marshall is one of a select few advisors who have been asked to work with more than 120 major CEOs and their management teams. He served on the Board of the Peter Drucker Foundation for 10 years. He has been a volunteer teacher for U.S. Army Generals, Navy Admirals, Girl Scout executives, and International and American Red Cross leaders, where he was a National Volunteer of the Year.

Marshall is the million-selling author of many books, including *What Got You Here Won't Get You There*—a *New York Times* bestseller, *Wall Street Journal* #1 business book, winner of the Harold Longman Award for Business Book of the Year, and top 10 bestseller in seven major countries; *Succession: Are You Ready?*—a *Wall Street Journal* bestseller; *The Leader of the Future*—a *BusinessWeek* bestseller; *The Organization of the Future 2*—Choice Award (top academic business books) 2009; and *Coaching for Leadership*. His last book, *MOJO,* was released in February 2010. It is a *New York Times* and *Wall Street Journal* top 10 bestseller, and the *Shanghai Daily* #1 business book in China.

More than 300 of his articles, interviews, columns, and videos are available for viewing and sharing online (for no charge) at www.MarshallGoldsmith Library.com.

Don Brown

Don Brown dedicates his career to sales and influence effectiveness—period. Bilingual and experienced at the executive and line level alike, you see the results of his work across dozens of industries, including brewing, automotive, airline, banking, and pharmaceuticals.

With more than 30 years working in the industry, Mr. Brown is heavily experienced in all phases of major performance systems implementation, from research and design to bilingual facilitation. Working with customers such as Anheuser-Busch, Dell Computers, Ford Motor Company, US Airways and United Airlines, Harley-Davidson Motor Company, Jaguar Cars, Compuware Corporation, SYKES, and Hilton Hotels, Don is accustomed to working domestically and internationally across all functional disciplines.

Mr. Brown has just released the newly developed *Multi-Touch Performance*™ products and services. Based on his own in-depth customer research and the premise that it takes several touches to learn, to teach, to sell, and to lead, Don has integrated the best of the best into a powerful sequence for human skills development.

As the owner of Situational Services, Incorporated, Don considers his work and mentorship under Paul Hersey and Marshall Goldsmith as the solid foundation of his success. Affiliated with Dr. Hersey for more than 25 years, Don coauthored *Situational Service*®—*Customer Care of the Practitioner* with Paul, and has worked hand in hand with him to create several highly successful training programs, including Leadership in a Team Environment, Situational Selling®—creating Readiness to Buy, and Performance Readiness®. Don also takes great pride in his long-standing customer relationships as well, some running over 20 years.

Don earned an honors degree from Michigan State University in foreign languages and a masters in management with Dr. Hersey at California American University. Don also lived and studied at the University of Seville in Spain, and works regularly in English and Spanish in Europe and Latin America. He lives in Ann Arbor, Michigan, and can be reached directly at Multi-Touch Performance.Com.

Bill Hawkins

Bill Hawkins is an expert in leadership development and executive coaching. He is a founding member of the Marshall Goldsmith Group and has worked with more than 20 Fortune 500 companies in 17 countries. Bill has designed and facilitated leadership education workshops for corporate clients on five continents. He also coaches leaders individually to increase personal effectiveness. Bill began his career with a division of Johnson & Johnson. He then joined Boston Scientific as director and then vice president of sales and marketing. With his blend of consulting and corporate management experience, Bill brings a breadth of understanding and insight to real-world situations.

Bill's clients include Acushnet, American Express, Ashland, AT&T, Bloomberg, Boeing, Boston Scientific, Budget Rent a Car, CalPERS, Cisco, ChevronTexaco, Cox Enterprises, C R Bard, Credit Suisse First Boston Bank, DirecTV, Dreyer's Grand Ice Cream, Exelon, Federal Reserve Bank, Ford Motor Company, FTI Consulting, GlaxoSmithKline, Hitachi (America), Internal Revenue Service, Johnson & Johnson, Labatt Breweries, Kodak, Kerzner International, KPMG, Las Vegas Metro Police Department, Marathon Oil Company, Martha Stewart Living, Mead Johnson, MGM–Mirage Hotels, Motorola, New York Stock Exchange, Nortel, Northrop Grumman, Oracle, Pfizer, PNC Bank, Raytheon, Sanofi-Aventis, Sterling Jewelers, TaylorMade-Adidas, Texas Instruments, Toyota, Union Pacific Railroad, Washington Mutual Financial Services, and Weyerhaeuser.

Aside from his work with major corporations, Bill has donated his services to the International Red Cross/Red Crescent, the New York Association for New Americans, and the Girl Scouts of the U.S.A.

Bill holds a BS from Drake University and an MBA from Indiana University. He is member of the Peter Drucker Foundation "Thought Leader's Forum," a Distinguished Fellow at the "Global Leadership Development Center" at Alliant University, and is listed in Who's Who in International Business. He is a contributing author in the Peter Drucker Foundation book *The Organization of the Future* (Jossey-Bass, 1997). He is also a contributing author in *Coaching for Leadership* (Jossey-Bass, 2003), *Change Champion's Fieldguide* (Best Practice Publications, 2008), and *What Got You Here Won't Get You There in Sales* (McGraw-Hill, 2012).